# From Marx to Williams

DIWAKAR REGMI

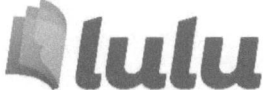

# From Marx to Williams

## An introduction to Marxist literary criticism

---

Imprint: Lulu.com

ISBN: 978-1-304-26660-6

# Preface

The idea of writing this book came suddenly one day when I was lecturing undergraduate students in the university. The prescribed textbook was Lois Tyson's *Critical Theory Today*. The brief essay on Marxism increased the appetites for Marxist literary theories in the students. They had many questions about Marxist perspectives on art and culture but I had only a few answers. I realized the necessity of compiling the thoughts of great writers and thinkers in a simple way, through paraphrase, along with some important quotations. The book was born around a year after its conception.

It is not a complete book; many great contributors to Marxist literary criticism have not been included in it. The theorists included here represent distinct fields of culture like art, literature, media, film, education, and ideology. Only the selected works of selected theorists have been paraphrased and quoted in the book. I hope this book will be a helpful guide to the beginners of Marxist literary criticism as well as to those interested in Marxist aesthetics and progressive literature.

I beg the reader's pardon for all the weaknesses in the book.

Diwakar Regmi

14 August, 2021

Itahari, Sunsari

# Contents

# I

# Introduction

Marxist literary criticism has been an intrinsic part of critical theory in the syllabus of almost every University around the world. Communist states in Europe formed under the premises of Marxism collapsed before they achieved their defined goal but Marxism as a critical theory has still been a popular theory among the literary critics, intelligentsia, and academia. The reasons are many and varied. Marxism as a critical theory is different from communism as a form of government although the premises of communism have quite a lot to do with the premises of Marxism. Unlike the critical theories preceding Marxism as well as those following it, Marxism is not only about interpreting the text in terms of its authentic values: its form, imagery, irony, plot, figures of speech, and the like. Marxism is concerned more with 'what' than 'how'. It is largely based on the belief that literature is all about ideas and the ideas are all about change and progress. Marx's belief that the theories, hitherto propounded, have interpreted the world whereas the aim of Marxism is not merely to talk about the world but to change it (*The German Ideology* 571) justifies the same. It is the reason why the revolutionaries and progressive intelligentsia have always adored the Marxist critical theories.

Marxism believes that "the economic situation is the basis" (Engels 294) on which society rests. "The production of ideas, of conceptions, of consciousness", say Marx and Engels, "is at first directly interwoven with the material activity and the material intercourse of men—the language of real life" (*The German Ideology* 42). The system of production and reproduction determines the overall aspect of human life: behavior, attitude, interests, motives, inclination to art and culture, and even a person's worldview. They elaborate the idea yet further:

The phantoms formed in the brains of men are also, necessarily, sublimates of their material life-process, which is empirically verifiable and bound to material premises. Morality, religion, metaphysics, and all the rest of ideology as well as the forms of consciousness corresponding to these, thus no longer retain the semblance of independence. They have no history, no development; but men, developing their material production and their material intercourse, alter, along with this their actual world, also their thinking and the products of their thinking. It is not consciousness that determines life, but the life that determines consciousness. (*The German Ideology* 42)

Literature, thus, cannot escape the economic realities. The simple songs of the pre-agrarian and agrarian man were different from the songs of the feudal societies. The post-modern literature at the climax of capitalism does not have anything similar to the literature of the Middle Ages. The literature of antiquity and the post-modern literature are as much different as the condition of the ancient caveman and the condition of the post-modern city dwellers. The post-modern literature produced especially in economically advanced capitalistic countries is more sensual than real. They appeal emotionally arousing sensual pleasure and excitement rather than appealing the readers for a change, informing them about the real condition of the world they live in and of their complicated lives amid the dialectics of development and regression, illusion and reality, virtual world of sensualism and the real world of commodification and so on.

Capitalism has always advocated for a free market economy. But the market has never been free; it is largely monopolized. The advocacy of a free competitive market has given birth to a vulgar economy. Broker capitalism has given birth to the idea of earning easy money which has created conditions more terrible than the conditions under the feudal societies. Human labor has, at large, been valueless, and the laborers have been subject to humiliation. A terrible form of slavery exists in the rich cities. The capitalist governments have covered their sad face with colorful masks.

Monopoly in production and distribution has increased the economic gap between the rich and the poor. Means of production and the entire market have been a prerogative of the handfuls. Privatization has gone rampant in every field of the economy leaving the poor at odds, at wonder, at fear, and a loss of humanity. The governments have merely been puppets at the hands of few who run the market. Education, health, sanitation, nutrition, art, and literature have all been run, managed, controlled, and monitored by private companies and organizations. It is not the people, but the market that elects the senators and the members of parliament. The people have merely been turned into the rabbles, just an instrument, a tool. The market has put them below the level of human beings.

The fall of the USSR has made the capitalists stronger than ever before. They have now got a readymade statement about the inefficacy of communism. With its newfound strength capitalism is striking hard on the poor, the mass and the voters. Capitalism has given the people their right to education but has robbed them of their schools, it has given them a right to life but has robbed them of their hospitals, it has given them the right to liberty and happiness but has robbed them of their choice and children. Instead of nutrition, it has supplied them with dust, CFCs, carbon dioxide, and other poisonous gases. It has robbed them of their brooklets, the rivers, the small farms, and crafts. The small entrepreneurs and artisans have been robbed of their traditional professions, and, instead, they have been shown a never-reaching destination of the better and smarter technocratic world. The capitalists argue the world of their dream is possible. Their argument bears truth in the sense that the destination they talk about has already been possible, but only for a few money-grabbers.

That the bourgeois can always keep the indigenous ethnic communities as their subordinate, they keep praising their cultures but despise the people. The cultures of the indigenous communities have been commodified; they are kept in an exhibition, and the bourgeois expresses the pride of being the owner of these cultures but never practices them himself. The real practitioners mostly live behind the curtains. As the real producers of crops in the feudal societies went through hunger and terrible death, the real producers of cultures have largely been isolated and alienated from their products. The indigenous groups have neither been able to come out to the markets nor are they in their previous state. They have been robbed of everything: their language, cultures, way of life, and fundamental human qualities. The bourgeois emphasis on the 'cosmopolitan character' of production and consumption has affected not only the local economy but also language, culture, and literature as well. As result, "from the numerous national and local literatures there arises a world literature. " (Marx and Engels, *The Manifesto* 13). The indigenous people even in the developed nations are in such a state that they can neither rise nor sit; they are compelled to stay in the half-sitting postures with many aches in their backs and limbs. The destruction of the communes of the indigenous people in the remote villages due mainly to the bourgeois quest for virgin land for merry-making, for business, for the establishment of construction companies, and industries, for fun-parks and swimming pools, has robbed the ethnic communities of their agricultural and pastureland, making most of them homeless ones. The bourgeoisie's accusation on the communists of intending to abolish private property is baseless since most of the private property has already been abolished, and whatever remains falls largely on the hands of the bourgeois class.

The modern bourgeois has been the sole producer and distributor. It has replaced the existing values and moralities with its own values and moralities. The bourgeois morality is teaching the people a new language, a new code of conduct, a new way of life, a new model of consumerism, in short, a new bourgeois morality. A terrible form of imitation prevails among the poor, the ethnic groups, the working-class people, the proletariat, and the subaltern – an imitation of consumerism, an imitation of bourgeois morality. The bourgeois tunes demand bourgeois dancing steps and the whole proletariat, being a slave to circumstances, and ideology is compelled to shake its hip to the bourgeois tunes. Human values like brotherhood, love to neighbors, love to community and nation have been mocked, and, in its stead, the bourgeois has installed the doctrine of competition, the free spirit, and individualism resulting in family breakdown, indifference, and alienation. "The bourgeoisie", write Marx and Engels, "has torn away from the family its sentimental veil, and has reduced the family relation to a mere money relation" (*The Manifesto* 11). The notion of competition has uplifted handfuls at the cost of the dehumanization of millions. Cooperation among the members of the community has been replaced by a new model of business. The market has pervasively got into people's kitchens, rituals, and human relations.

Different breakthroughs in science and technology have paved the way for the learned middle-class people to oppose the bourgeois ideology. A great number of middle-class youths today are being atheists. But most of the poor working-class people have been hegemonized by the agents of the bourgeois with the false hope of heaven. The poor are taught to prepare not for their rights, but death and postmortem rites. The Bible, the Quran, and the Purana – all of which are the sources of bourgeois ideology – are still being taught to the poor working-class people. A large amount of money is being spent every year in the slums and ghettos of poor countries for the erection of temples, churches, and mosques, and these places sanctioned by the bourgeois as the holy places, have been crowded with people, mostly the uneducated, the poor and the working-class. That the hunger can be overcome by devotion, that the sick can be healed by devotion, and that sorrows can be overcome by attending the preachings of certain pundit, or a clergyman, or a mullah, is the very old bourgeois model of exploitation that still exists in the poor workers' societies.

The form of domination and exploitation has been changed. The bourgeois has made them more severe and stronger than ever before. Hegemony has been an unseen and disguised form of domination and exploitation. The cosmetic life of the proletariat in rich modern cities may shine radiantly with his fashionable clothes, branded cars, and mobile phones, but under the cosmetic life dwells the real, the sad, the hegemonized proletariat. He has been made compelled to live in such a situation by the bank installments, the housing policies, the insurance policies, and the complete complicated maze of bourgeois economy. Revolting against the system means loss of jobs and opportunities. With noble schemes and policies, the bourgeois has bought the proletariat so that they cannot revolt against the system.

Democracy, the idea of the free press and personal liberty, has been a tool to rob the proletariat. Election in the modern bourgeois democracy has largely been a kind of business of the bourgeois. Voters are either threatened, intimidated, blackmailed, or bought.

The members of parliament are mostly the representative of interest groups, corporate houses, business tycoons, mafias, or brokers. The farmers, laborers, and intellectuals, i. e., the representatives of the people, rarely get an opportunity to get to the parliament. The latter groups are usually used as instruments, in the parliament, they are mocked, humiliated, or harassed. The real issues of the marginalized and the working-class are rarely discussed in the parliament. Such issues are discussed only if they benefit the bourgeois.

The notion of democracy and free press has only been a myth so far. The media has never been free. The kings and the courts used them, or rather misused them, to suppress the voices of the marginalized, and today they have been managed and run by the bourgeois to suppress the proletariat. Instead of informing the people, the media are selling news. Bernard Shaw's remark "Money talks: money prints: and money broadcasts" (VIII) aptly characterizes the media in the bourgeois democracy. The self-stuck label on the media as the fourth organ of a state has been a license of the bourgeois to hegemonize the working-class. The ads, commercials, soap operas, and even the current-affair programs and talk shows are designed in the interest of the bourgeois. Hegemony works as a slow poison, and before the proletariat realizes the effects, he finds his cultures buried deep under the bourgeois ideology.

The biggest irony of the modern-day bourgeois economy can be seen in the political system and the political parties. The bourgeois democrats are never tired of talking about freedom of choice but bar the people from choosing a party of their own. The communist parties have usually been labeled as anti-nationalistic or terrorist organizations. Such parties are either banned or are kept under the strict vigilance of the bourgeois security. The so-called democratic parties set by the bourgeois are mostly like the private companies of the handfuls established on the bourgeois investment to rule the working-class. Such parties bear the same ideology, are established for the same purpose, but bear different names, and are run by different individuals. The working-class people do not have access to these parties; they cannot afford to join them and chair some significant posts. Few of them may be nominated, but only for escaping public blames. The bourgeois parties run their own media, control and manipulate information, feeding the people with their fake information so that they can reserve votes for the next election.

Capitalism has accelerated the rate of migration from the remote villages to the cities, or from the poor countries to the rich ones. Marx and Engels write vividly in *The* Manifesto:

> The bourgeoisie has subjected the country to the rule of the towns. It has created enormous cities, has greatly increased the urban population as compared with the rural, and has thus rescued a considerable part of the population from the idiocy of rural life. Just as it has made the country dependent on the towns, so it has made barbarian and semi-barbarian countries dependent on the civilized ones, nations of peasants on nations of bourgeois, the East on the West. (13)

While the villages are emptied of people and economic activities, the cities and towns are overcrowded and polluted. Poverty has been damaging more lives in the towns than in the villages. Under the pretext of making a city, the bourgeois is rampantly establishing *bazaars*, the markets, and in them, the bourgeois has made everything a commodity: art, cultures, sports and sportsmanship, literature and the authors have been the private properties of the corporate houses.

The rich countries, in the similar way, are robbing the poor ones of their bona fide citizens. The skilled, the learned, and the well-informed ones are being traded these days by the *manpower companies* to the rich countries since they easily acquire a visa and a PR. While the poor countries are struggling due to the lack of expert human resources, the rich ones are rejoicing in the discovery of new talents. The USA, Canada, and Australia, among others, are doing progress at the cost of brain drain in the African and Asian countries. The universities and the workplaces in these countries are crowded with expatriates. The system of visas has barred the poor ones from traveling whereas it has been an entrance to the rich ones to further riches. The majority of the people, the farmers, and the workers have almost nothing to do with the visa.

Many people today believe that Marxism is an outdated political and philosophical model. They argue that the Marxist system has never existed, that the communist system in the USSR and other eastern European countries was mostly oligarchic, and the true working-class has never been in power even in the communist countries. The claims bear little truth in them. But it does not mean that the Marxist theory is outdated and, therefore, it is to be rejected. Marxism as a philosophical system has contributed to society and the world more than any other philosophical system has done. It has been successful in raising political consciousness in the working-class people, in women, in the marginalized races, and the traditional ethnic groups. Its strength lies in setting up labor unions, in the various independence movements, in the democratic revolutions, in anticolonial movements, and in analyzing history, art, and cultures. It has been one of the most accurate tools to analyze political history, the market, and conflicts around the world. Marxism, as a scientific mode of thought, has taught people to escape the false hope of heaven and the burden of the divine. It has taught people to respect labor. Marxism is still relevant and will remain so forever.

Before going to the discussion of Marxist critics and their criticism, it is essential to discuss several premises of Marxism. The Marxist idea of the economic base and the superstructure are helpful for a student of Marxist critical theory. The idea, in brief, implies that the base of a society is its economy, that is, the entire system of production reproduction, and distribution. On the economic foundation lies the social, political, ideological, or cultural superstructure. The stronger the base is, the stronger the superstructure becomes, and a change in the economic base results in the change of superstructure. Marx clarifies the relationship between the base and the superstructure in the preface of *A Contribution to the Critique of Political Economy*:

> In the social production which men carry on they enter into definite relations that are indispensable and independent of their will; these relations of production correspond to a definite stage of development of their material powers of production. The sum total of these relations of production constitutes the economic structure of society - the real foundation, on which rise legal and political superstructures and to which correspond definite forms of social consciousness. The mode of production in material life determines the general character of the social, political and

spiritual processes of life. It is not the consciousness of men that determines their existence, but, on the contrary, their social existence determines their consciousness. (11-12)

This metaphorical representation of society as a building is a critique of Hegel's idealism, but, more than that, this metaphor today has been an important tool to understand the character of a society, including art, culture, and literature. Although some of the latter Marxist critics have some reservations about the idea, which we shall discuss later, it implies that the faculty of human language and the production of literature as well lies in the ideological superstructure and that a change and development in the material base brings a change in them. The relationship between the base and the superstructure works the other way as well; a change in the superstructure demands a change in the base, too. For example, the rise of political awareness among the working-class people makes them revolt against the system, thereby destroying the economic base to construct another one, yet stronger, capable of holding the enlarged superstructure. The base and the superstructure, thus, have a reciprocal relationship; a change in one brings a change in the other.

This metaphor has given birth, though Marx did not use the term himself, to the idea of historical materialism, which has become a buzzword among the Marxists. The idea implies that "the basis of society and of social change is production or productive activity" (*A Historical Dictionary of Marxism*). The economic condition for the Marxists is the material circumstance whereas the product of the material circumstance, like social, political, ideological, or cultural phenomena is a historical situation. Marxist thinkers believe that no event in the political history of a country can be understood without an understanding of the material circumstance. This idea of the interpretation of history has been one of the most important tools for literary critics, historians, anthropologists, and feminists. A Marxist literary critic, thus, analyzes the text in the light of the material circumstance the text was produced in because the production of the text is just a historical situation resulted from the economic condition of the time.

Marxism is a practical scientific political as well as social theory. It believes that every theory should apply to real-world situations.

In other words, Marxist praxis evaluates political or socio-economic theory based on its applicability to real-world situations. The theories like idealism and mysticism, for Marxism, are far from the real-world situation. The Marxist praxis directs the historians, theorists, literary writers as well as critics to look at events and activities with precision and accuracy.

The Marxist idea of class division and class struggle are equally important to the student of Marxist literary criticism. The world has been divided in different ways: there are divisions based on religion, caste, race, gender, and so on. The division of people based on class is more significant than any other division for the Marxists. Marx presents a survey of the history of class division and struggles between them in various epochs. In capitalism, the division is between the bourgeois and the proletariat. Marx and Engels, thus, explain in *Manifesto of the Communist* Party:

> In the earlier epochs of history, we find almost everywhere a complicated arrangement of society into various orders, a manifold gradation of social rank. In ancient Rome, we have patricians, knights, plebeians. slaves; in the Middle Ages, feudal lords, vassals, guild-masters, journeymen, apprentices, serfs; in almost all of these classes, again, subordinate gradations.

> The modern bourgeois society that has sprouted from the ruins of feudal society, has not done away with class antagonisms. It has but established new classes, new conditions of oppression, new forms of struggle in place of the old ones.

> Our epoch, the epoch of the bourgeoisie, possesses, however, this distinctive feature: It has simplified the class antagonisms. Society as a whole is more and more splitting up into two great hostile camps, into two great classes directly facing each other - bourgeoisie and proletariat. (9)

The former in the Marxist division are the ones who own the means of production like lands, organizations, factories, industries, and resources including human resources. The latter, on the other hand, has nothing of its own. This class includes working-class people like factory workers, miners, construction laborers, and so on. Marx believes that there is a constant struggle between two classes sometimes overtly and sometimes covertly. In the long run, in a decisive struggle, the proletariat emerges victorious and sets up the dictatorship of the proletariat, abolishing all the private properties and division between the classes.

Marxism dictates that literary creation is a product of material circumstances. It is about the people of a time, about their relations, their struggles and achievements, their motives, and their living conditions. A Marxist critic studying a certain character, let's say, in a folk tale, finds that the character's actions and activities are historical situations produced by the material circumstances of the time. He studies whether the character stands for oppressor or the oppressed. Not only physical intimidation, but the character might also have been psychologically, mentally, or emotionally oppressed or harassed. A Marxist critic studies whether the character is aware of the fact that he is being oppressed or not, whether he is a revolting type or not. In progressive literature like Gorky's *The Mother*, the characters are politically informed and are revolting types. The Marxist idea of class and class struggle is, therefore, significant to students of critical theory.

In modern cities, it is difficult to place people under only the category of proletariat or bourgeois. The manufacturing industries are mostly run by machines. The small artisans have been replaced. There are, instead, shopkeepers, small entrepreneurs, and so on. Where shall we place these people? Marx and Angels give a solution for this problem as well. The names of the classes may be different ones in different epochs but there have been, and there will always be two hostile classes; the exploiters and the exploited, or the oppressor and the oppressed.

That the proletariat or the oppressed can be dominated easily, the bourgeois has created many arbitrary divisions. The divisions of caste, religion, race, sects, creeds, genders are all the creation of the minority, i.e., the ruling class, to oppress the majority and to make their reigns stronger. Women, for example, know that they are oppressed irrespective of their religion, caste, or race, but they cannot be united under an umbrella union due to other many folds of divisions. It is the same with the working class as well. Therefore, the Marxists feel a need for a vanguard communist party that can, through the extension of its organization, unite all the oppressed and wage a revolution against the entire bourgeois system. Lenin writes in *What is to be Done*, "Only a party that will organize real all-national exposures can become the vanguard of the revolutionary forces in our time" (85). The task of such a communist party, according to Lenin, will be to organize a universal political struggle. To achieve this goal, the party must train "Social-Democratic practical workers to become political leaders, able to guide all the manifestations of this universal struggle, able at the right time to "dictate a positive program of action" for the discontented students, for the discontented Zemstvo, for the discontented religious sects, for the offended elementary school teachers, etc., etc" (82).

The Marxist concept of ideology is the most important mine for a Marxist critic to dig out the meaning of a literary text; a literary text is the storehouse of the author's ideologies, and also that of the society that the text is produced in. An author uses diction, symbols, and other figures of speech to convey his ideologies to his readers. Ideology in Marxism means a belief or a system of beliefs. Hindu's belief that eating beef is a sin is as much an ideology as a Muslim's belief of the same about pork; a Marxist's belief that economy is the base on which the superstructure is built is as much an ideology as a capitalist's belief that competitive free market determines a country's economic development. Thus, the idea of command economy as well as the free economy, and communism, as well as individualism, are ideologies.

Marxism demands that we should be able to distinguish between regressive and progressive ideologies in a text. It is equally important for a Marxist literary critic to find out and analyze the repressive and non-repressive ideologies in a text. Marxism believes that the beliefs commonly practiced for a long time are the product of the material circumstances of a time. Ideologies are tools to repress the people. The Hindu belief and practice of the system of caste, for example, is an ideology conditioned by the material circumstance in which the king, the Kshatriya, and his priest, the Brahmin, put themselves on the top and the Vaishyas, the business class, and the Shudras, the manual workers, on the bottom. Different stories, myths, and jokes were made about this division of caste in such a way that the people believed the division a divine sanction and that a breach of the code of caste was subject to punishment by the king, the Brahmin as well as the God. A similar form of ideologies prevails in all the religions of the world. Such repressive ideologies are merely an invention of the oppressor to oppress the people.

Oppressive ideologies are sanctioned not only by the ruling class to oppress the ruled ones but also by the patriarchate to exploit the women. The idea that women are naturally inferior to men is a sexist ideology reared by patriarchy. Almost all the religions of the world have conditioned such ideologies to dominate women. The Bible's story that Eve was created out of Adam's rib, that Eve was responsible for man's fall; Islam's code that a man can have four wives at a time, that a woman should wear *burka*; that the Hindu's practice of *sati* and the worship of *linga*, and so on are all repressive ideologies.

The bourgeois ideology like 'competition' and 'individualism' has been proved more damaging to the socialist and communist system. These ideologies have been the license of the few to exploit the majority. While the majority struggles for the stomach, the majority piles up the world's property. The ideas like 'survival of the fittest' and 'will to power' have been the bourgeois' buzz words. The poor, on the other hand, are compelled to believe that they are poor either because they failed to compete or because of some sins they had committed in their previous life. They try to falsify the first assumption by their speedy labor, which ultimately serves the bourgeois' interest in speedy work, and the second one by being devout. The working class, thus, cannot involve in revolutionary activities due to fear of loss of job. He knows he is being exploited but is compelled to be so. It is the ideology that has made him a slave to circumstances. Therefore, Marx and Engels ask the working class to unite and fight the bourgeois system as the proletariat has nothing to lose in the struggle, but the world to win *Manifesto of the Communist Party* 44).

Marxism demands that the ideologies are to be tested based on material circumstances and historical situations. All ideologies are not oppressive ideologies. The empirical or the scientific ones are progressive ideologies. Marxism as an ideology is a progressive ideology in that it is based on science. The ideologies like patriarchy, individualism, competition, free market, consumerism, and so on are false consciousness. These ideologies are merely the tools for those in power to dominate and exploit the ruled ones.

One of the purposes of a Marxist critic is, then, to find the ideologies in art, literature, music, dance, theatrical performance, cinema, television commercials, and other cultural productions. The Marxist literary critic should be aware of the role of ideologies in certain literary texts- whether the ideologies serve the interest of the ruling class, whether they are oppressive, whether they support the socio-economic system, or they are the bearers of revolutionary ideals. The ideologies in a text help not only to understand the author's psychology but the ideals of the time as well.

Marxism demands the study of the effects of growing industrialization on an individual and a society. Before industrialization had started in Europe, small artisans produced their own brand of products. For example, while an artisan named 'A' was famous for making spades another one named 'B' was famous for his caps. They had earned their identity themselves. They were present in their products. But after the rise of industrialism, the small artisans and farmers lost their identities. The factories replaced their business. The factories of mass production employed laborers, but it was impossible to identify a laborer from his labor and product. Marx writes that in industrial capitalism "the worker is related to the product of his labor as to an alien object" (*Economic and Philosophic Manuscripts* 71). Such labor in marxism is called alienated labor. The laborer is alienated from his own labor as well as from the product he produces. Marx thus elaborates the idea:

> The more the worker spends himself, the more powerful the alien objective world becomes which he creates over -against himself, the poorer he himself - his inner world - becomes, the less belongs to him as his own. It is the same in religion. The more man puts into God, the less he retains in himself. The worker puts his life into the object; but now his life no longer belongs to him but to the object. Hence, the greater this activity, the greater is the worker's lack of objects. Whatever the product of his labor is, he is not. Therefore the greater this product, the less is he himself. The alienation of the worker in his product means not only that his labor becomes an object, an external existence, but that it exists

outside him, independently, as something alien to him, and that it becomes a power on its own confronting him; it means that the life which he has conferred on the object confronts him as something hostile and alien. (71-72)

Capitalism has commodified everything. The value of everything is determined in terms of money. Even human beings have been commodified. The workers in various fields of life sink to the level of a commodity becoming "indeed the most wretched of commodities" (*Economic and Philosophic Manuscripts* 69). For Marxism, an object or a person, or an idea becomes a commodity when it gains a monetary value. Marx talks about two types of value in *Capital*: the use-value and the exchange-value. "The usefulness of a thing", he writes, "makes it a use-value" (126) but "it is only by being exchanged that the products of labor acquire a socially uniform objectivity as values, which is distinct from their sensuously varied objectivity as articles of utility" (166). The second value is the exchange value. For example, in addition to the use-value of a piece of land, that is to grow crops, it has exchange value, that is to sell it. The exchange value of a commodity has made it more mystical, something that is entirely detached from its producer, something that is revered like an idol possessing magical power. Marx calls such a magical tendency of a commodity 'commodity fetishism'.

Capitalism is always in quest of new commodities and new markets: new commodities to compete with the existing products, and new markets to sell the commodities. This quest has resulted in building empires across the oceans giving birth to imperialism, which, in Marxism means cultural, military, political, or economic domination of a more powerful country over a less powerful one. For example, the need for a market brought British capitalists to India. Gradually they wielded more power on the Indian nationalities, ultimately making India a part of their empire. In *Manifesto of the Communist Party*, Marx and Engels have pointed out how the bourgeois quest for a new market gives birth to imperialism:

The discovery of America, the rounding of the Cape, opened up fresh ground for the rising bourgeoisie. The East-India and Chinese markets, the colonization of America, trade with the colonies, the increase in the means of exchange and in commodities generally, gave to commerce, to navigation, to industry, an impulse never before known. (9-10)

Capitalism, through its practice of imperialism, colonizes not only nation and people but also human consciousness. Colonization of consciousness takes place when the imperialist persuades the people in the colonial country that they are inferior to the colonizers, not only in power but also in their culture, values, economy, and religious practices. These were the tools that the European immigrants used against the native Americans and the British against the Indians.

Marxism is a dynamic theory of growth. Marxist ideas on literature have been propounded by many Marxist critics after Marx and Engels. The ideas are many and varied but they have all contributed to the development of Marxist politico-economic thought as well as Marxist literary criticism. In the following chapters, we shall discuss the individual contributions of some prominent Marxist critics and theorists of Marxist literary criticism.

# II

# V. I. Lenin and the Study of Contradictions in Tolstoy's Works

Lenin contributed to the development of Marxism by applying Marxist theory into practice, mainly by organizing people of different walks of life under a vanguard communist party that led a revolution to establish a communist regime in Russia. Many of his organizational models, like democratic centralism, are still in use among the communist parties. Besides, he wrote widely on various subjects related directly or indirectly to political, social, and cultural revolutions. Although we do not find any prescriptive text by Lenin on art, aesthetics, and literary criticism, his ideas on the role of art in the life of people and society can be generalized from his writings on Leo Tolstoy. His writings on Tolstoy are at the same time, criticism of the literary giant, observation of the contradiction in the then Russian society, and, covertly, suggestions to the revolutionary artists on Marxist aesthetics.

Lenin reads the contradiction of the Russian society and the weaknesses of the Russian revolution in the contradiction of Tolstoy's books. "The contradictions", says Lenin, " in Tolstoy's works, views, doctrines, in his school, are indeed crying"(6). On the one hand, he finds Tolstoy to be a literary genius criticizing social hypocrisy, capitalist exploitation, governmental violence, farcical courts, and so on with sober realism; but on the other, he finds him to be preaching religion and clericalism. Such contradictions in Tolstoy, for Lenin, are not accidental; they are the reflections of the contradictions of the Russian societies in the last third of the 19th century when foundations of the peasant economy were shaking, and capitalism was raising its head. Lenin believes the contradiction in Tolstoy's works has to be judged from such a standpoint of rising capitalism.

As a prophet, Lenin finds Tolstoy to be ridiculous. But as an expresser, he finds him to be the original writer who has penned down the features of the Russian revolution as a peasant bourgeois revolution. In this sense, the contradictions in Tolstoy's views are a mirror of the "contradictory conditions under which the peasantry had to play their historical part "(7) in the Russian revolution. The whole of the peasantry in Russia, according to Lenin, was aware, very naively of the situation at hand. They were unhappy with landlordism and tsarism but they had no idea about the kind of revolution and revolutionary principles that could answer them. Very few of the peasantry participated in the revolution; most absconded from it. They wept and complained and chose to remain servile to the bourgeois instead of joining the revolutionary proletariat. Thus, for Lenin, "Tolstoy's ideas are a mirror of the weakness, the shortcomings of our peasant revolt, a reflection of the flabbiness of the patriarchal countryside and of the hidebound cowardice of the 'thrifty muzhik'"(8).

Lenin believes that the appraisals of Tolstoy presented by both the governmental as well as liberal newspapers are blemished and misleading ones. They have made vain appraisals not based on facts but based on sentiments to the great author. The former shed their crocodile tears and vow to respect Tolstoy, but at the same time, prompt to defend the 'Holy' synod that "excommunicated Tolstoy" (13). Similarly, the appraisals of the literary genius by the liberals, for Lenin, are empty as they use the vapid and threadbare phrases to praise him – phrases that Tolstoy fiercely castigated. The only appropriate way of appraising Tolstoy, therefore, is to read his books from the standpoint of the social contradictions that he presents.

It is necessary to know the historical material situation to understand the relationship between Tolstoy and the working-class movement in Russia. Tolstoy was writing in the period between 1861 and 1905, when serfdom still existed and when its vestiges "thoroughly permeated the whole of the economic (particularly rural) and the whole of the political life of the country" (15). This period also witnessed the growth of capitalism from below and its promotion from above. At this time, the agriculture of Russia was in the hands of ruined and impoverished peasants who practiced absolute and primitive farming and husbandry. During the same time, when the influence of world capitalism was increasing in Russia, the peasants began to suffer the most. They either starved to death or were condemned to migrate to the urban areas, developing with new possibilities of capitalism abandoning their land in the country. According to Lenin, "it was this rapid, painful, and abrupt collapse of all the old 'foundations' of old Russia that found reflection in the works of Tolstoy the artist, in the views of Tolstoy the thinker"(16).

Lenin critically observes the place of Tolstoy's doctrine in the proletarian struggle. He believes that Tolstoy vigorously castigated the ruling classes and exposed the falsity of the social institution of the time like the church, the courts, militarism, bourgeois learning, and so on. It does not, however, mean that he was writing on the proletariat cause. Rather, his doctrine contradicted the life and struggle of the revolutionary proletariat. Lenin puts it vividly that Tolstoy was the spokesman of the vast mass of people who hated the masters of the Russian society but who had not realized the necessity of an uncompromising struggle against them. This mass of people, says Lenin, stood between the ones that wanted to defend the old order and the ones that wanted to destroy it and looked puzzled during that historical hour of revolution. This mass was fed up with the old order and wanted to find an escape, but did not have a definite solution.

Despite all these reservations about Tolstoy Lenin believes that the literary giant can still be relevant to the Russian working-class and revolutionaries. By studying Tolstoy's works, says Lenin, the Russian working-class can know its enemy better. From his books, he says, "the entire Russian people must learn wherein lay their own weakness, which prevented them from consummating the cause of their emancipation. This must be learned in order to make progress"(18). However, the Russian people, he says, will achieve emancipation only when they learn from the proletariat not from Tolstoy.

Lenin believes that to understand the meaning of Tolstoy's works we need to understand the characteristics of the Russian society of the time when he was writing. The mere sugar-coated words in his praise would only be superficial and far detached from reality. Tolstoy seems to know the nature of the society when he makes Levine in *Anna Karenina* say, "but among us now everything has been turned upside down and is only just taking shape"(26). What has been turned upside down is the old order, the order of the feudal system, the serfdom; but what is taking shape was beyond Tolstoy's conjecture. Regarding what was taking shape, Tolstoy reasoned only in the abstract. Tolstoy recognized "only the standpoint of the 'eternal' principles of morality, the eternal truths of religion failing to realize that this standpoint is merely the ideological reflection of the old ("overturned") order, the feudal order, the order of the life of oriental nations"(27). This is where the biggest contradiction lies in the works of Tolstoy who seems to have noticed the characteristics of the society but fails to accept the historian's ideas of progress; and, instead, advocates the oriental ideology of asceticism and pessimism.

Lenin's criticism of Tolstoy can be summed up in a few lines: he holds that Tolstoy portrayed the Russian life as it was, that the contradictions in his books were the contradictions of the period and that he knew the falling old order, but regarding the course of events, he stood at odds. Tolstoy knew the suffering of the people but failed to acknowledge the real cause of suffering and a way out of it. Lenin seems to suggest that a revolutionary author should, in addition to depicting the real contradictions of a time and the real suffering of the people, be able to depict the real causes of contradictions and suffering along with a solution to them in a revolutionary way.

# III

# Leon Trotsky and the Spirit of Anti-Formalism

Leon Trotsky is not only a veteran communist leader of the USSR but also a classic Marxist thinker and Marxist literary critic. His work *Literature and Revolution* has been a milestone in the history of critical theory. In the book, Trotsky places the role of art in general and literature in particular above all other social and cultural practices that contribute to the development of socialism. In the book, he writes against formalism, futurism, and all other forms of writing that do not uphold the proletarian cause and the cause of the revolution.

Trotsky believes that the solutions to the very basic problems of mankind like foods, clothes, lodging, and education are not enough to uphold the historic principle of socialism. Only the movement of scientific thought and the development of new art can uphold the principle. For him, "the development of art is the highest test of the vitality and significance of each epoch" (29).

Trotsky believes that different forms of art developed along with the development of society. The ruling class has always dominated art. like other ideologies, art has been a production of the ruling class. The old literature and culture of Russia before the revolution, for example, were the expressions of the noblemen and the bureaucrats. Though the literature of the time was based on the peasants, the life and the problems of the peasants were told through

21

the perspective of the noblemen. After the literature of the noblemen, arose the literature of the intellectual commoners, which was based on the peasants and the bourgeois. The intellectual commoners gradually grew "modernized, differentiated and individualized" (30). This change made them focused on different new forms that emphasized the aesthetic elements more than on the problems of life. By the end of the 19th century, the intellectual commoner had converted to the bourgeois intelligentsia. The new art developed after the revolution disrupted the bourgeois center. The art in such epoch, after the workers' or the people's revolution, centered only on the people without the bourgeois. By the term people, Trotsky means "the peasantry, to some extent the small burghers of the city and after that those workers who cannot be separated from the protoplasm of peasants and folk" (30).

Even after the revolution, Trotsky believes, there remains a division between physical work and intellectual work. Physical work, among others, includes revolution which can be led only by the workers; and intellectual work, among others, includes the production of art and literature. As the revolution is the expression of peasants and workers, art is the expression of the intellectuals who hesitate between the peasant and the proletarian and who are incapable organically of merging either with one or the other, but who gravitate "more towards the peasants" (30). He says that one of the aims of the revolution is to overcome the division of physical work and intellectual work, and this can be done by constructing socialist culture, in which the new art, "realistic, active, vitally collectivist, and filled with a limitless creative faith in the future" (33), will arise.

Trotsky is a critic of the idealists who believe that the mind or the knowledge leads the world. The idealists put the mind before the world and experience. Trotsky argues that a man, throughout the day, involves himself in labor, in movement, in different events, or enjoys nature, and that experience gives a shape of the ideas he develops later. Expression of art in such a way is realistic, is true to life and experience. He believes that the Russian literature before the revolution was unrealistic and far away from the expression of the people, but still, such literature can be manure for the new culture.

Trotsky finds a transitional art between the pre-revolution bourgeois art and the new art which is yet to be born. He calls the litterateurs of this transitional phase the 'fellow travelers' of the revolution. The transitional art, he says, "is more or less organically connected with the Revolution, but which is not at the same time the art of the Revolution" (61). The 'fellow travelers' could not have become litterateurs without the revolution. They were not revolutionary themselves, neither they did belong to the 'changing landmarks' group, which implied a break with the past or the convention or radical change of front. The literature of the 'fellow travelers' was the product of the revolution. They accepted revolution in their own way but the communist ideal, in the true sense of the word, was not theirs. Trotsky, thus, writes, " If non-October (in essence anti-October) literature is the moribund literature of bourgeois land-owning Russia, then the literary work of the "fellow travelers" is, in its way, a new Soviet populism ... without political perspective" (62). For, the 'fellow travelers' were not the artist of the proletarian revolution.

Trotsky is a critic of futurism as well. He finds, in futurism, a bohemian origin. He criticizes the futurists for being asocial, nonpolitical, individualistic, and for their lack of respect for old values. He says that the futurists' break from the past or the old value may have liberated them from the old bourgeois cultures but such a break from the past cannot address the working class, as the latter cannot break with literary tradition. That is to say, the futurists' call for a break from tradition has put them in a closed circle of the intelligentsia. In contrast to the futurists, Marxists live in traditions without ever being deviated from revolutions. He explains:

> We elaborated and lived through the traditions of the Paris Commune, even before our first revolution. Then the traditions of 1905 were added to them, by which we nourished ourselves and by which we prepared the second revolution. Going farther back, we connected the Commune with the June days of 1848, and with the great French Revolution. In the field of theory, we based ourselves, through Marx, on Hegel and on English classical political economy. We were educated, and we entered the struggle during an organic epoch, and we lived on revolutionary traditions. (Futurism 4)

He, thus, summarizes the differences between the communists and the futurists as the political revolutionist and the revolutionary innovator of forms, and as the one stepping into the revolution and the one falling into it.

Trotsky is, however, optimistic that futurism has a possibility of rebirth, or of entering into the new art as an important component. He believes "they are the necessary links in the forming of a new and great literature" (Futurism, 25). But for this, futurism has to remove its mask of the intelligentsia, and when it does so futurism will no longer be futurism.

As a critic of Russian formalism, Trotsky finds formalism to be standing in opposition to Marxism. Formalism is connected closely with futurism but the difference is that while futurism "was capitulating politically before communism, formalism opposed Marxism with all its might theoretically" (The Formalist School, 1). He opposes radically the propositions of the formalists propounded by its head, Viktor Shklovsky, that "art has always been the self-sufficient pure forms" (The Formalist School, 1). By declaring form to be the essence of poetry, he says, formalism "reduces its task to an analysis (essentially descriptive and semi-statistical) of the etymology, and syntax off poems, to the counting of repetitive vowels and consonants, of syllables and epithets" (The Formalist School, 2). Addressing Shklovsky's destruction of Marxism in five points, he argues that the formalists failed to realize that literature is a socio-economic product. It, however, does not mean that the socialist project is to dominate art by the means of decrees and orders. On the other hand, it says that art is a product of socio-economic conditions or material circumstances. The Marxists do not dictate that the art should speak only of the workers or the factory chimney or the uprising against capital. The new art places the struggle of the proletariat in the center. The pain of the artist can cover a broad and wide area, with a feeling of newness and a new consciousness of the new man. Trotsky seems to have similar ideas about literary works to that of T. S. Eliot expressed in the famous essay "Tradition and Individual Talent". Addressing Shklovsky, Trotsky writes:

> "Yes, themes migrate from people to people, from class to class, and even from author to author. This means only that

the human imagination is economical. A new class does not begin to create all of culture from the beginning, but enters into possession of the past, assorts it, touches it up, rearranges it, and builds on it further. If there were no such utilization of the "secondhand" wardrobe of the ages, historic processes would have no progress at all". (The Formalist School, 12)

He writes that a critic cannot always use Marxist theory to decide whether to accept or reject art or literature. Instead, a work of art should be judged or evaluated by the law of art itself, but it is only the Marxist theories that can precisely say why, how, and by whom a certain tendency in art was developed in a certain historical situation. That is to say, only historical materialism can explain the birth of a certain type of form of literature at a certain time.

Trotsky believes that in each epoch the ruling class has always been the creator of art and culture. The lifestyle of the ruling class, their customs, and costumes music and literature, in short, their production of culture, in general, becomes the culture of the state. The feudal slave-owning cultures in the Middle Ages and the bourgeois culture in capitalism are its examples. Does it mean that after the establishment of the dictatorship of the proletariat followed by the proletarian revolution led by the vanguard party, there will be the creation of proletarian cultures? Trotsky believes that there is no such possibility of the creation of a proletarian culture since the creation of culture requires a long time. The bourgeois, for example, has come into power for around 500 years. The bourgeois cultures had begun to be created even before the bourgeois came into power. The proletariat, however, will have a very short period to rule as the dictatorship of the proletariat is just a transition between the proletariat revolution and the establishment of the socialist system.

Trotsky believes that the proletarians cannot create their class culture as the bourgeois, and even the noblemen before them did because the proletarians have to involve themselves in the revolution which goes through class struggle. During the struggle, says Trotsky, there will be more destruction than the construction of culture. And by the time the revolution is over, the proletariat as a class begins gradually to dissolve into a classless social community, and, thereby, ceases to be the proletariat. In such a rapid transition no new culture can be created; the one created after the establishment of the socialist system will have no class character.

Another reason why the proletarians will not have their own proletarian culture is that the proletariat revolution is anti-class in its nature and purpose. That is to say, the proletariat wages revolution not to create a class culture but to annihilate it to create a new human culture. He writes that the dictatorship of the proletariat is not an organization for the production of the culture of a new society but a military system struggling for it. The new human culture, however, does not emerge out of chaos; it will continuously grow out of the old culture. Trotsky suggests that one should learn from his enemies too, and for the development of new human culture, the proletariat has to, first of all, take into its hands the apparatus of culture like the industries, schools, publications, press, theaters, and so on.

Trotsky talks about the relationship between the communist party and the production of art and cultures. He says that the law of social attraction to the ruling class is applied in the field of art as well. Such a tendency has been seen in the USSR as well after the revolution. Such a law of social attraction is not harmful, for it is not true that only the workers create revolutionary art. The working class has a greater inclination to political movement than to art and literature. They have to go through a series of struggles, strikes, demonstrations, and even violence. They have almost no time to produce art. The contemplative intelligentsia, on the other hand, is politically passive. History of revolution around the world shows that they hardly go directly to strikes and struggles in the same way as the workers and the peasants do. Therefore, they have more time for contemplation and `artistic reproduction of revolution.

Trotsky discusses the role of a communist party in the field of art. He answers the question of what the position of the party should be concerning the production of art. He believes that the communist party should not dictate art. It should not hold an eclectic position in the matter related to the production of art. He writes:

> Marxian method affords an opportunity to estimate the development of the new art, to trace all its sources, to help

the most progressive tendencies by a critical illumination of the road, but it does not do more than that. Art must make its own way and by its own means. (Communist Policy Toward Art, 2)

He further says that the party leads the proletariat but does not dictate the historic process. It does not, however, mean that the party allows every form of art to grow; it repels the poisonous and disintegrating tendencies of art since such art is regressive and reactionary.

Trotsky as a political theorist says that the communist party has to pay little attention to the development of art since it has other more vital political businesses. He accepts that the party is less protected on the flank of art, and also science than on the political front. He writes, "We ought to have a watchful revolutionary censorship, and a broad and flexible policy in the field of art, free from petty partisan maliciousness" (Communist Policy Toward Art, 5). He gives a hint on how a communist party can contribute to the development of progressive art. He says that the establishment of schools in villages resulting in increased literacy following the proletariat revolution will give access to the peasantry to art and literature. The working class in the cities cannot have time and resources for the production of literature, but the peasantry, after its contact with the literature of the intelligentsia, can produce art. Trotsky writes that such an indirect union between the workers of the city and the peasants of the village can produce historically progressive art. This will, thereby, strengthen the cooperation between the village and the city, pave the way for the movement of the peasantry to socialism.

Trotsky's idea on revolutionary art and its difference from socialist art, which is yet to come, can also be important for a student of Marxist critical theory. About revolutionary art, he finds two kinds of artistic phenomena: the first of which means those works that speak about the theme of the revolution, and the second stands for those works that are colored by the new consciousness arising out of the revolution. He believes that revolutionary art should not be mistaken for socialist art. For, revolutionary art is about all the contradictions of a revolutionary social system and serves as the transition for the production of socialist art.

Revolutionary art contributes to the purpose and strength of revolution because it promotes the consolidation of the workers in their struggle against the exploiters.

Trotsky answers Nietzsche who believed that socialism, like Christianity, belittles a man through its scheme of leveling down, ultimately changing a man into a herd animal. Trotsky writes that solidarity does not degenerate man but elevates him. Art has so far been a prerogative of the rich or the noble class and caste. But with the solution of the basic problems of man, and with the end of class-antagonism, the creative man will be able to look up to art, enjoying it and producing it. The men of creativity, no matter what caste they belong to, will involve themselves in creation, developing art, and, at the same time, exalting themselves to a height.

Trotsky writes about the birth of the theatre, its role, and its development in the present time. He writes that theatre is the most creative form of art which requires a new realistic revolutionary repertory. He says that instead of staging the play of the previous generation, there is a need of staging the plays encompassing the events and enthusiasm, the dreams, and the achievement of their own time and place. He writes, "A new class, a new life, new vices, and new stupidity, demand that they shall be released from silence, and when this will happen we will have a new dramatic art, for it is impossible to reproduce the new stupidity without new methods" (Revolutionary and Socialist Art 9 ). He places a higher value on tragedy than on comedy. He believes that tragedy is a great and monumental form of literature. He looks at the development of tragedy from the perspective of historical materialism. The tragedy of classic antiquity was deduced from the myths and had the theme of fate, whereas the tragedy of the medieval period dealt with the theme of god, church, or heaven. The tragedies of these periods had nothing to do with the real problems of human beings in general-nothing to do with dialectical materialism.

He gives higher value to the tragedies of William Shakespeare. He says that in the plays of Shakespeare, one finds that the fate of the ancients and the religious pessimism of the medieval Christians are crowded out by individual human passions such as love, jealousy, revenge, greed, and so on. Shakespeare's art, he says, is more human than that of his predecessors, and even in modern times, art revolves, more or less, around similar themes. He writes that even in socialism, tragedy will get its room. Socialist art, he says, will revive tragedy, but without the god. The new art will be atheist. It will revive comedy as well because the new man of the future will want to laugh. According to him, socialist art will give new life to the novel and grant all rights to lyrics as well.

Trotsky's main concern in *Literature and Revolution* lies not in the aesthetic pleasure that a literary work serves, but the acceleration of the proletariat revolution. He believes that the urban workers cannot produce literary works due to a lack of time as they have to keep themselves busy in the physical works including the revolutionary ones. Therefore, the intellectuals belonging to the country peasantry should supply them with revolutionary literature inspiring them to struggle against the bourgeois system. Thus, he demands a union of the country peasantry and the urban proletarians for the accomplishment of the revolution. He believes that this union should work even after the revolution for the establishment of the classless socialist society.

# IV

# Georg Lukacs and Socialist Realism

Georg Lukacs's career as a literary critic began as early as 1914 when his critical theory was published. The book *Theory of Novel* was not written in the tradition of Marxist literary criticism. In it, we find a strong influence of Hegel. He admits it in the preface to the later edition in 1962 when he says, "It was written in a mood of permanent despair over the state of the world" (12). It was 1917, the October Revolution, that answered the problems that seemed insoluble to him. By 1920 he had been a member of the communist party, and since then he enriched the Marxist critical tradition with many critical, theoretical, political, as well as ideological works.

Lukacs' views on literature began to be shaped with an insight into the Marxist worldview soon after he joined the communist party. We can find a clear Marxist influence in his brief review of the Indian poet and novelist Rabindranath Tagore's novel *The Home and the World*. In the review entitled "Tagore's Gandhi Novel", Lukacs dismisses Tagore as a creative writer, calling his celebrity among Germany's intellectual elites as one of the cultural scandals. He finds Tagore an insignificant writer as his creative power is non-existent, his characters pale stereotypes, his stories threadbare, and sensibility meager. For him, the novel is a collection of quotations from the *Upanishads* and *The Bhagavata Gita*, but not a creative text. He calls Tagore an intellectual agent of the British and the Nobel Prize a reward for his service. For, instead of lauding the native freedom fighters, he "attempts to conceal his impotent hatred of the Indian freedom fighters in a profound philosophy of the universally human". India was going through the brutality of imperialism, but instead of raising questions against it, Tagore is concerned with the question of spirituality and eternal truth. In this sarcastic review, we see Lukacs growing up with Marxist critical tradition.

"Eulogy for maxim Gorky: A Great Proletarian Humanist" written in 1936 shows the maturity of Lukacs as a Marxist critic. While Trotsky was passionately waiting for socialist culture and art to develop out of the revolutionary cultures and art, Lukacs finds Gorky a precursor of socialist realism and proletarian humanism. For Lukacs, Gorky stood in a unique historical position since he was a friend and companion of Tolstoy as well as Lenin. This is the reason that made Gorky's works unique. Although Gorky was a contemporary of the period when realism was on the verge of decline in Europe with the advent of naturalism and formalism, Gorky was not affected by the decline. Instead, he continued with the traditions of the old realists like Tolstoy. Lukacs writes about the similarities between Tolstoy and Gorky:

> Like Tolstoy, Gorky was charged with a tremendous humanistic indignation against the degradation and sophistication of man by feudalism and capitalism. His was a glowing, un-vacillating and consuming humanistic passion for human integrity, for an ideally well-rounded and fully developed man. Gorky carried this fire to the real leaders of the exploited and oppressed, to the revolutionary proletariat. The glow of indignation he blew to a Promethean flame of revolution.

Lukacs finds Gorky taller than all the revolutionary writers of the time. While other writers writing about the struggle of the proletariat for emancipation limited themselves to the picture of political struggles leaving humanism merely as an abstract idea, Gorky manifested the actual effectiveness of humanism in the revolutionary labor movement. Talking about Gorky's works, he says:

The labor movement awakens and develops, gathers and organizes the human forces of each one who takes part in it. It is in and by means of the labor movement that distorted, crippled men turn again into human beings. It gives back the power of speech to the dumb, sight to the blind. It wrests mankind from the clutches of dullness, through which can be seen only what is present and direct. Inasmuch as it shows men the future, it also illuminates their past and brightens the present, making it full of purpose-of-conscious struggles. It shatters the barriers erected by capitalism to separate man from man and unites them in the most human way, in a common struggle.

Unlike other revolutionary writers, Gorky shows victims, failures as well as the breaking of human bonds by the cruel necessities of the struggle. Such a portrait of life during the revolution has made him a great proletarian humanist and his works belong to the school of socialist realism.

"Realism in the Balance" written in 1938 is one of the most influential essays of Georg Lukacs that belongs to the tradition of Marxist Literary Criticism. The essay critiques Expressionism, Impressionism, Naturalism, Surrealism, and other avant-garde modern schools of literary theories, and advocates realist literature. Lukacs finds three main currents in the literature of his time, which are not entirely distinct, but rather overlap in the development of individual writers: anti-realist or pseudo-realist literature, avant-garde literature, and realist literature. Among these trends, writes Lukacs, realism is in the balance as far as progressive trend is concerned.

The essay is a defense of realism as well as an answer to Bloch's objection to Lukacs' ideas of 'totality' and 'unified reality'. He writes that the ideas of totality and unified reality have nothing to do with other schools of literary criticism, but they are essential for a Marxist realist. He says that the modern literary schools of the imperialist era, whether it is naturalism or surrealism, has one thing in common, that is:

> They all take reality exactly as it manifests itself to the writer and the characters he creates. The form of this immediate

33

manifestation changes as society changes. These changes, moreover, are both subjective and objective; depending on modifications in the reality of capitalism and also on the ways in which class struggle and changes in class structure produce different reflections on the surface of that reality. It is these changes above all that bring about the swift succession of literary schools together with the embittered internecine quarrels that flare up between them. (1040)

The problem with these schools of literature, according to Lukacs, is that they remain frozen in their own immediacy both emotionally and intellectually without being able to pierce the surface to discover the underlying essence. In other words, they fail to relate their experiences to the hidden social forces that produce them. Instead, these schools develop their own style of spontaneous expression to present their immediate experience.

The realists, on the other hand, do not confine themselves to their own immediate experience. According to Lukacs, the major realists of the era have been successful in "abandoning and transcending the limits of immediacy, by scrutinizing all subjective experiences and measuring them against social reality" (1040). The basic difference between the realists and other schools of literature of the time lies in the fact that the latter are immaterial and one-dimensional. They do not rise above the level of immediacy. Lukacs accepts the fact that without abstraction there can be no art, but abstraction must have a direction. Abstraction for the sake of abstraction makes art one-dimensional. Unlike the naturalists, surrealists, and impressionists, the major realists fashion:

> . . . the material given in his own experience, and in so doing makes use of techniques of abstraction, among others. But his goal is to penetrate the laws governing objective reality and to uncover the deeper, hidden, mediated, not immediately perceptible network of relationships that go to make up society. (1041)

As these relationships do not lie on the surface, and as the realists have to dig out them from the deeper level of the objective reality, the work of the realists requires both intellectuality and art. This is the reason, unlike the schools of literature mentioned above, realism has both artistic as well as intellectual dimensions. He calls this realistic venture artistic dialectic of appearance and essence. He says the richer this dialectic is the more firmly it grasps hold of the living contradictions of society, thus, making realism greater and more profound.

Lukacs attacks the expressionists calling them more ideologues who stand between the leaders and the masses. They were, like the immature revolutionary masses, confused and uncertain about their own convictions. Lukacs says that they were influenced by reactionary prejudices of the age and were susceptible to various anti-revolutionary slogans like abstract pacifism, the ideology of non-violence, abstract critiques of the bourgeois, and all sort of other anarchist notions. The ideological influence of expressionism discouraged the process of revolutionary clarification among its followers, instead of promoting it. As a result, when the revolutionary masses in the Soviet Union became mature and the realists had a stronghold among the masses with its clarity about the objective reality, the ground on which expressionism and other avant-garde literature stood began to crumble.

Lukacs is also a critic of modern popular art. According to him, the theories of modern popular art, being influenced by avant-garde ideas like ruptures, fissures, catastrophes, abstraction, and discontinuity, have pushed the realism of folk art into the background. He sounds like Trotsky when he rejects the idea of the abrupt discontinuity of tradition. He maintains that since the life of the people is a continuum, it cannot be accepted that revolution means merely discontinuity. History, for him, "is the living dialectical unity of continuity and discontinuity, of evolution and revolution" (1055). At the same time, there is a question of cultural heritage too. Since cultural heritage has a living relationship to the people, the artist has to be able to understand the roots of the relationship. Mere ruptures are not the solution. Lukacs believes that only the realists, since they are the children of the people, can understand the roots of the relationship and portray the relation in art.

Lukacs' longer volume *The Historical Novel* can be read as his own correction to his ideas about the novel in his earlier book *Theory of Novel*, not simply because it covers a broad area of subject matter and more mature premises, but also because it follows the Marxist call for dialectal materialism for the development of history. Written in 1937, the book begins with a discussion of the classical form of the historical novel. He analyses the social and historical conditions for the rise of the historical novel. His survey of the development of the novel traces the beginning of the historical novel at the beginning of the 19th century, in Sir Walter Scott's novel *Waverley.* He writes that the novels with historical themes were written in the 17th and the 18th century as well but those novels before Scott lacked "the specifically historical, that is, derivation of the individuality of characters from the historical peculiarity of their age"(19).

The classical form of the historical novel, primarily that of Scott for Lukacs is an epic, representing the human type of an Age, and a place whose lives are swayed to and fro by various socio-economic forces. Such novels dealt with the life of a famous historical figure, but their lives, action, and ideas are conveyed not directly through themselves but through the characterization of some intermediate type of person around whom the narrative revolves. Such intermediate types of characters, according to Lukacs, stand between the opposing forces, that is, the leaders or the historical figures and the masses. Marx and Engel's views on the progressive nature of history have been reiterated slightly in different words in Lukacs' book. He means to say that the classical historical novels present a conflict between the ascending and descending social forces or classes in which the losers are honored whereas the historical necessity of the winners is upheld. In doing so, a historical novel upholds the sense of progress. For Lukacs, the classical historical novel is a precursor to the realistic novels of the 19th century. The democratic humanism of the 20th century, in a way, follows from certain characteristics of classical historical novels. He finds Balzac and Tolstoy to be the heir to Scott since they have served as a transition to democratic humanism.

Since historical novels emerged at about the time of Napoleon's collapse, one needs to pay attention to what social and ideological bases contributed to its arrival. Lukacs analyses many factors including the Enlightenment, the new humanism, and historicism. Scott's novels, for Lukacs, are not flash floods, not an absolute break but the direct continuation of the great realistic social novel of the

18<sup>th</sup> century. The historical novel was born in England because England was more fertile for its growth as England had had a post-revolutionary character at that time after the bourgeois revolution before any other European country.

Lukacs fears that Scott's sense of history may be mistaken for the Romanticists' sense of history. For him, however, these two contrast each other in that Scott " lets his important figures grow out of the being of the age, he never explains the age from the position of its great representatives, as do the Romantic hero-worshippers" (39). In other words, Scott's historicity was focused on the 'below to up' model while the romanticists' was focused on the 'up to below' model. Thus, the historical conception of romanticism is diametrically opposed to that of Scott since the latter gives a perfect artistic expression of the basic progressive tendency of the period.

Lukacs believes that nobody before Scott had such a sense of history that the being of an Age can be presented as a many-sided picture only if the everyday life of the average people, their joys and sorrows, their crises and confusions are portrayed. For him, an only retelling of great historical events does not make a novel historical one but the poetic awakening of the people who figured in those events is more important. The historical novels should make us experience different motives that led men to think, feel, and act as they did in historical reality because it is the law of literary portrayal that to bring out the social motives of behavior, the outwardly insignificant events are "better suited than the great monumental dramas of world history" (42).

It is also important to note that Scott's novels, according to Lukacs, share the general epic functions present in the Homeric epics as well. As Homer has lifted Achilles from his surroundings very genuinely by epic means, which are both artistic and true to nature, so has Scott done to his heroes.

Lukacs writes that every writer is a child of his age, that is, his works are the product of socio-economic conditions of the time he writes. It follows that the historical novelists of the era of the anti-Imperialist, anti-Fascist, and democratic movement got the subjects of their novels in the socio-economic as well as political systems of the time. He, thus, sums up, "The objectivity of a great writer depends upon an objective and, at the same time, living involvement with the major tendencies of social development" (275). He further writes, in the line of *The Communist Manifesto* that partisanship, too, grows organically out of the struggle of historical forces in the objective reality of human society.

Lukacs' essay "Existentialism" written in 1945 is a critic of Heidegger, Husserl, and Sartre. It examines the development of existentialism as a philosophical current among bourgeois intellectuals. He does not find existentialism an epoch-making new philosophy. He says that "an epoch-making philosophy has never yet arisen without a really original method". He gives examples of Plato, Aristotle, Descartes, Spinoza, Kant, and Hegel, all of whom gave mankind an epoch-making philosophy due to originality in their method. But Existentialism does not have originality in its method basically for two reasons: first, it is an offshoot of Husserl's philosophy, and second, Husserl's philosophical 'third way', the injunction of essence beyond idealism and materialism, is flawed in its very conception, and, at the same time, beyond originality. Lukacs, thus, settles the dispute over the originality of Husserl's alternative 'third way':

> Is there any room for a "third way" besides idealism and materialism? If we consider this question seriously, as the great philosophers of the past did, and not with fashionable phrases, there can be only one answer, "No." For when we look at the relations which can exist between being and consciousness, we see clearly that only two positions are possible: either being is primary (materialism), or consciousness is primary (idealism). Or, to put it another way, the fundamental principle of materialism is the independence of being from consciousness; of idealism, the dependence of being on consciousness. The fashionable philosophers of today establish a correlation between being and consciousness as a basis for their "third way": there is no being without consciousness and no consciousness without being. But the first assertion produces only a variant of idealism: the acknowledgment of the dependence of being on consciousness.

He means to say that phenomenology is a development of idealism in another way. The invention of the philosophical 'third way', for him, is a product of the imperialist period because, he says, men can hold themselves to be thorough-going idealists only in troubled times.

The phenomenological method, says Lukacs, claims to have discovered a method of knowing, which exhibits the objective reality of essence without going beyond human consciousness. But for Lukacs, such an abstract narrowing of reality, or an idealist distortion of the problem of reality is intentional deceit; it is nothing more than fetishism.

What influenced the development of existentialism as a philosophical theory? Lukacs finds that after the philosophy of phenomenology, the growing interest of the bourgeois intellectuals in nihilism, pessimism, and fetishism gave birth to existentialism as a philosophy. The existentialists, for him, find life losing its meaning. The characters in literary works raising existential issues portray men who have lost the center, or the connectedness of their own lives. What makes the writers portray life this way? Lukacs answers, "The man who lives in the fetish-making world does not see that every life is rich, full, and meaningful to the extent that it is consciously linked in human relations with other lives". Nietzsche's nihilism and irrationalism and Heidegger's concept of nothingness are the results of fetishism.

Thus, existentialism, which has developed out of Husserl's philosophical 'third way' and has been influenced by Heidegger's concept of nothingness is the philosophy of death and abstract freedom. About the material circumstance leading to this historical situation, Lukacs says that Heidegger was writing on the eve of fascism whereas Sartre was writing at the daybreak of democracy. That is to say, Heidegger saw only nothingness whereas Sartre saw only freedom. The fusion of the concept of nothingness and the individual choice of freedom is what has come to be called existentialism. For Lukacs, however, the Sartrean concept of freedom is a bankrupt idea. Sartre's scorn for social viewpoints and public life makes his concept of freedom abstract and irrational.

Such an idea of freedom revolves around nothingness and nihilism and gives ideological support to the individualists.

In the essay "Nietzsche as the Founder of Irrationalism", Lukacs observes how Nietzsche's philosophy developed out of the revolutionary and counter-revolutionary movements of the time. He writes that Nietzsche was writing on the eve of Imperialism. He had seen the conflicts of Bismarck's age, the founding of the German Reich, the inauguration of aggressive imperialism by Wilhelm II, the Paris Commune, the origin of the proletarian parties, and the outlawing of the socialists. Such material circumstances gave birth to Nietzsche's irrationalism.

Lukacs finds, in Nietzsche, a Jekyll-and-Hyde character. He writes that Nietzsche "waxes enthusiastic if the revolutionary character of his discontent receives a philosophical sanction, but is at the same time deflected — with regards to its social substance — into a rebuttal of democracy and socialism" (316). Lukacs believes that Nietzsche worked with the sixth sense; he never read Marxism, neither did he understand economics. These are the reasons that he was hostile to Marxism calling it a herd morality that levels down individuals. For Lukacs, Nietzsche was concerned only with the super-structure of society, not with its base.

Lukacs' chief contribution to Marxist literary tradition is his idea of socialist realism. He rejects expressionism, existentialism, nihilism phenomenology, and every other avant-garde artistic movement as he finds them deviated from the objective reality of the world. His idea of socialist realism demands a writer to get deeper into the objective reality and serve it aesthetically. It is, thus, a fusion of art and intellectuality.

# V

# Antonio Gramsci and the Formation of the Intellectual

Italian communist, leader Antonio Gramsci, has in recent years been a popular name among the Marxist literary critics basically for his ideas on the formation of intellectual, his concept of education, the subaltern class, and hegemony. These ideas will briefly be discussed here.

Gramsci clearly states the nature and types of intellectual along with their function in society. He believes that all men are intellectuals in themselves but all men do not have an intellectual function in society. So, Gramsci's ideas on intellectual rest on this dialectic between being intellectual and playing intellectual function in society. He argues we call somebody intellectual but we cannot call anybody unintellectual because each human being uses intellect. The entrepreneurs do have a certain category of intellect and even the menial laborers use intellect along with physical force. He writes that purely physical work independent of intellect does not exist.

Based on social function, Gramsci classifies intellectuals into two types: organic intellectuals and traditional professional intellectuals. The organic intellectual implies various strata of intellectuals that are historically created and that explicitly takes the side of a certain social group or a class that creates it. Gramsci writes:

> Every social group, coming into existence on the original terrain of an essential function in the world of economic production, creates together with itself, organically, one or more strata of intellectuals which give it homogeneity and an awareness of its own function not only in the economic but also in the social and political fields. (5)

For example, the capitalist creates a technical workforce along with specialists in political economy, new legal systems, and so on. The capitalist entrepreneur himself possesses a certain type of intellectual capacity like the organization of the mass of the workers, certain technical capacity, and the like. The new class that is coming into dominance has a challenge of the expansion of its class by elaborating its cultures and general system of relationships. For this, the capitalists must choose their deputies from among the employees. This also helps in the creation and elaboration of the organic intellectuals yet further. Such intellectuals created and elaborated organically uphold the interest of the class that creates it. Otherwise, there begins a crisis in the class. For example, the feudal lords possessed a technical military capacity, and when they began to lose this intellectual capacity, the bourgeois began to come into prominence which, thereby, created and elaborated its own organic intellectuals.

Gramsci believes that the classes coming into prominence, whether feudal or the bourgeois, draw the intellectuals from another class, mostly from the dominated one. He says that the peasantry supplies the dominant classes with organic intellectuals who then cease to be linked to the class of its origin. The peasantry does not elaborate its own organic intellectuals. Gramsci's implications are clear here; while the dominant class like the bourgeois draws organic intellectuals from outside its class, the proletarians, in course of their development, have the challenge to create, elaborate, and retain the organic intellectuals from within its own class.

The traditional professional intellectuals, on the other hand, represent the category of intellectuals that is not, like organic ones, elaborated by the class coming into dominance. Rather, this category of intellectuals according to Gramsci "is already in existence which seemed indeed to represent an historical continuity uninterrupted even by the most complicated and radical changes in political and social forms" (7). For example, the priestly class like Ecclesiastes in the Christian societies and the *purohits* in the Hindu societies existed before the bourgeois revolution and continue to exist in bourgeois capitalism. This category of intellectuals has still a significant influence on the ideological systems like education, religion, cultures, and the like. The traditional professional intellectuals claim to be autonomous and independent of any social group but, for Gramsci, they cannot be independent. For example," the category of ecclesiastics", says Gramsci, " can be considered the category of intellectuals organically bound to the landed aristocracy" (7). That is to say, the traditional type of intellectuals assimilates gradually to the class that comes into dominance.

Gramsci does not mean that only the dominant social group forms the intellectuals. Instead, he believes that each of the social groups forms the specialized category of people for the exercise of intellectual function. But with the dominant social group, the intellectuals gain more and quicker elaboration. Moreover, the dominant class tends to assimilate and conquer the traditional intellectuals into itself, and this process is simplified if the class in question can elaborate its own organic intellectuals. For Gramsci, the social classes use schools as an instrument for the function of the elaboration of various levels of intellectuals. The levels of intellectuals and their variation depend on the number and type of schools. The classical schools produce, for example, state functionaries and professionals whereas the technical schools produce technicians for the industries. The role of the dominant class remains dominant in the use of the school as an instrument for the production of intellectuals because the dominant class, which possesses the institute of higher cultures, more easily assimilates into the education system. When the intellectual is, thus, historically formed by the dominant class with a purpose, explicit or implicit, to uphold the values of the class in question, the intellectual becomes "the dominant group's 'deputies' exercising the subaltern functions of social hegemony and political government" (12). Thus, for Gramsci, the intellectual is an instrument of social hegemony.

Along with the distinction between the organic and traditional intellectual, Gramsci distinguishes between the rural and the urban intellectuals, in which the latter types, in a way, overlap the former types. The intellectuals of the urban-type have grown along with the growth of the industries. Industrialization requires technicians, organizers, and even the general staff. Such a need gives birth to more urban intellectuals. These intellectuals do not have their own autonomous independent roles. They can neither make any plan nor any decision. Their job is to execute the plans of the entrepreneurs. They are like the subaltern officers in the army, and their position lies between the instrumental mass and the entrepreneurs.

The rural intellectuals, on the other hand, are mostly the traditional type. Unlike the urban type, "they are linked to the social mass of country people and the town (particularly small town) petite bourgeois, not as yet elaborated and set in motion by the capitalist system" (14). These types of intellectuals have socio-political functions as they play an important role to bring the peasant masses into contact with the administration. The rural type of intellectual like the teacher or doctor lives comparatively higher standard of life, and in a way is a role model for the peasant masses who dream of making their children like them. The most interesting distinction between the rural and the urban type of intellectuals Gramsci makes is the one related to their role in society. As the rural type of intellectuals plays a significant political role and enjoys significant reputation and power, the urban-type is confined only to the factory works. The technicians do not exercise political function over the instrumental masses. Instead, sometimes, the instrumental mass exercises significant political functions over the technicians.

If the intellectuals cannot become autonomous or independent of the dominant groups coming into existence, what could be their role in politics and political parties? Gramsci answers vividly that the dominant group wields together the organic intellectuals and the traditional intellectuals. The intellectuals who join a particular political party merge themselves with the organic intellectuals of the party and are liked tightly with the party. Does it mean that the party has already had intellectuals before elaborating the organic intellectuals? Gramsci's answer is interesting as well as relevant. For him, all the members of a particular political party are functionally intellectuals since the nature of their work in the party is directive and organizational which, in itself, has an educative function.

Gramsci's ideas on education and the education system are equally important to a Marxist literary critic since the education system is closely linked to the elaboration of intellectuals, which, in turn, is linked to the elaboration of society, cultures, and economy. Gramsci believes that with the variation in practical activities of the modern people, there emerged a need to create a new type of school to produce specialists in the particular practical field. It has resulted in the establishment of two types of schools: the classical ones for the production of professional intellectuals and the vocational ones for the production of practical specialists. This differentiation and particularization, however, for Gramsci "is taking place chaotically, without clear and precise principles, without a well-studied and consciously established plan" (26), and is the chief cause of educational crisis today. For, such a division of vocational and classical school promotes class differences in societies, i.e., the dominant class and the intellectual send their school to classical school whereas the instrumental mass to the vocational ones. To minimize the rift between the dominant class and the instrumental mass, Gramsci suggests a different model of schooling, "a common basic education, imparting a general, humanistic, formative culture" which "would strike the right balance between the development of the capacity for working manually (technically, industrially) and development of the capacities required for intellectual work" (27). This enables pupils to choose a future career of their own interest and capacity.

Gramsci, in a similar way, talks about two types of activities developed alongside two types of schools: deliberative activities and technical-cultural activities, the latter of which has created the bureaucratic body, i.e., the body of functionaries. The creation of such functionaries, for Gramsci, has long-term political and economic consequences. He writes:

> This is one of the mechanisms by means of which the career bureaucracy eventually came to control the democratic regimes and parliaments; now the mechanism is being organically extended and is absorbing into its sphere the great specialists of private enterprise, which thus comes to control both regimes and bureaucracies. (27)

This mechanism which has come to dominate the regimes and bureaucracy involves the integration of the personnel specialized in political activities and the personnel specialized in technical activities. Such a tendency of the mechanism in question cannot be overcome by the systems and endeavors outside the mechanism. The traditional type of political leader fails to overcome such a tendency. He says, "The traditional type of political leader, prepared only for formal-judicial activities, is becoming anachronistic and represents a danger for the life of the state". Therefore, he suggests that the leaders should have "minimum of general technical culture which will permit him, if not to 'create' autonomously the correct solution, at least to know how to adjudicate between the solutions put forward by the experts, and hence to choose the correct one from the 'synthetic' viewpoint of political technique" (28).

Gramsci's prescriptive suggestions about the organization of common schools are, to some extent, relevant today. He writes that the aim of the common school, i.e., the one that teaches general humanistic cultures, should be inserting the youths into social activity after a certain age. The method of educating should entirely be public so that children can involve themselves in the process of education without a division of class or caste. For this, there should be an expansion of the practical organization of the school like the teaching body, laboratories, buildings, and so on. Since such an organization requires a large sum of money, in the initial stage, the new type of school should be "only for restricted groups, made up of young people selected through or recommended by similar institutions" (30). The primary level should exceed no longer than four years and the children should be taught about rights and duties along with the concept of the state and society, in addition to reading, writing, sums, and so on, so that they learn to ignore the folkloristic conception of the social environment. The rest of the school-going time should not exceed six years so that by the age of fifteen or sixteen children will have completed common school.

Gramsci finds a gap between the school and the university since there is a break in the passage from quantity to quality. He writes:

> From an almost purely dogmatic education, in which learning by heart plays a great part, the pupil passes to the creative phase, the phase of autonomous, independent work. From the school, where his studies are subjected to a discipline that is imposed and controlled by authority, the pupil passes on to a phase of study or of professional work in which intellectual self-discipline and moral independence are theoretically unlimited. And this happens immediately after the crisis of puberty when the ardour of the instinctive and elementary passions has not yet resolved its struggle with the fetters of the character and of moral conscience which are in the process of being formed. (31-32)

To bridge this gap between school and university, Gramsci suggests the provision and organization of 'creative' school as the culmination of the active school. Writing about the distinctions between these two phases, Gramsci says:

> In the [active] phase the aim is to discipline, hence also to level out - to obtain a certain kind of 'conformism' which may be called 'dynamic'. In the creative phase, on the basis that has been achieved of 'collectivization' of the social type, the aim is to expand the personality- by now autonomous and responsible, but with a solid and homogeneous moral and social conscience. (33)

This does not mean that an active school is a school of investors and discoverers, but one where learning is spontaneous and autonomous with the teachers working only as friendly guides.

Such creative schools, according to him, contributes to the development of society by producing responsible citizens no matter whether they join university and become intellectuals or become factory workers.

Gramsci's main argument is clear: he demands the establishment of a common formative school run by the state where all pupils irrespective of class and caste can attend and get free education. He is against the division of schools into classical and vocational types. The traditional schools too had their drawbacks; they trained the children of the ruling class, and, thus, were sources of hegemony. The vocational school becomes a school only for the instrumental masses. One may ask, "What is wrong with the vocational school that produces trained and skilled workers"? Gramsci scrutinizes this question through the lens of democracy. For him, only to make unskilled workers skilled is not the meaning of democracy. In a democracy, instead, the mass should get an opportunity to rise to the status of the governed given they have capacity and interest.

Gramsci's classification of the ruling class and the subaltern class is also useful for a Marxist critic. The chief disinclination between them lies in the matters related to unity in these classes. In the ruling classes, says Gramsci, we find a unity of political society and civil society, whereas the subaltern classes "are not unified and cannot unite until they are able to become a state". The history of the ruling classes is, for him, "the history of States and of groups of States", whereas the history of the subaltern classes "is intertwined with that of civil society, and thereby with the history of States and group of States" (52). Gramsci, in a nutshell, presents six phases of the birth of the subaltern classes and their journey to unity through the establishment of the communist party:

> 1. the objective formation of the subaltern social groups, by the developments and transformations occurring in the sphere of economic production ; their quantitative diffusion and their origins in pre-existing social groups, whose mentality, ideology and aims they conserve for a time ; 2. their active or passive affiliation to the dominant political formations, their attempts to influence the programmes of these formations in order to press claims of their own, and

the consequences of these attempts in determining processes of decomposition, renovation or neo-formation; 3. the birth of new parties of the dominant groups, intended to conserve the assent of the subaltern groups and to maintain control over them ; 4. the formations which the subaltern groups themselves produce, in order to press claims of a limited and partial character ; 5. those new formations which assert the autonomy of the subaltern groups, but within the old framework; 6. those formations which assert the integral autonomy, ... etc. (52)

The history of the formation of the communist party, i.e., the party of the subaltern group, is, thus, complex and zigzag since the history must include all the consequences of the activities of the subaltern parties on the global subaltern groups and the attitudes of the dominant groups. Moreover, the consequences of the actions of the dominant groups backed by the state must also be included in the history of the subaltern parties. The history should also study the hegemony exercised on the subaltern groups through the mediation of a party or any other hegemonic group. He gives an example of how various innovatory forces, developed from subaltern groups, defeated the dominant groups and led national Risorgimento in Italy. These forces eliminated or subordinated the dominant forces and won support from specific auxiliary forces, and, thus, became a state. For Gramsci, the elimination of the enemy groups and the support from the auxiliary groups are the yardsticks to measure "the level of historical and political consciousness which the innovatory forces progressively attained in the various phases" (53). If the level of the historical and political consciousness of the innovatory forces is measured only by the yardstick of their separation from the dominant groups, history becomes a unilateral one.

For Gramsci, "The history of subaltern social groups is necessarily fragmented and episodic" (54-55). They tend to unify but often their unification is interrupted by the activities of the dominant groups. And even if they unite and defeat the ruling class, they are anxious only to defend their success. Therefore, Gramsci suggests not an immediate but a permanent victory of the subaltern groups for which these groups have to develop and unite through the comprehensive historical cycle discussed above.

The study of the history of the subaltern groups and the subaltern parties can better be understood with Gramsci's concept of hegemony which is a tool of domination used by the dominant or the ruling class. Hegemony is like a slow poison to suppress the rebellious nature of the governed and involves ethical, political, and economic phenomena. For example, the ruling class develops many ethics, whether cultural, political, or economic, and convinces the governed to be adapted by the same. The religious institutions, schools, and the court are powerful apparatuses of hegemony. Moreover, all the three powers, legislative, judiciary, and executive, in which the unity of the state is manifested, are the "organs of political hegemony" (247). For Gramsci, hegemony has a universal character and exists as long as the economic classes exist, and as long as the societies are divided into civil society and political society.

# VI

# Walter Benjamin and Media Study

Walter Benjamin studies the transformation of various forms of art in general and visual art in particular in his essay "The Work of Art in the Age of Mechanical Reproduction". The reference to Marx as a prognostic philosopher in the preface of the essay is suggestive of the views in the essay being prognostic themselves. This has come true now after his essay has been one of the most important resources for media study. He puts forward the argument that the transformation is taking place due more to the developmental tendencies of art than to the desire of man.

Benjamin presents us with a brief history of the reproduction of human artifacts from Greek art of founding and stamping to modern sound film. Human artifact, for him, has always been reproducible but never before the advent of camera and sound film art was reproduced in such intensity. Because the innovative techniques of reproduction accelerated the speed of human perception. He writes:

> For the first time in the process of pictorial reproduction, photography freed the hand of the most important artistic functions which henceforth devolved only upon the eye looking into a lens. Since the eye perceives more swiftly than the hand Can draw, the process of pictorial reproduction was

accelerated so enormously that it could keep pace with speech. A film operator shooting a scene in the studio captures the images at the speed of an actor's speech. (1168)

As a result, by the beginning of the 20th-century technical reproduction of art reached such a standard that it could reproduce all the transmitted works of art, and made a room of its own among the artistic processes of various types and genres.

The most vital and innovative part of Benjamin's essay is his study of the effects of the reproduction of the work of art and the art of the film on the art in its traditional form. Every work of art has a peculiarity of its own, i.e., it is produced at a certain time and in a certain place. The technical reproduction, no matter how perfect it is, deprives the work of art of its one of the most unique existence, i.e., its presence in time and space. Both types of reproduction; process reproduction (film or photography) and manual reproduction (making a replica) rob the work of art of its 'aura', i.e., the authenticity and the aesthetic value.

Benjamin says that the insatiable human desire for adjusting the mode of perception along with the changes in the mode of their existence has paved the way for the invention of the techniques and technologies of reproduction of art. That is to say, human desire to bring art closer to the eyes has invented lithography, printing press, photography, and films. But due to this desire for the adjustment of perception, art is lacking in its aura. He says, "Unmistakably, reproduction as offered by picture magazines and newsreels differs from the image seen by the unarmed eye. Uniqueness and permanence are as closely linked in the latter as are transitoriness and reproducibility in the former" (1171). The uniqueness of art, similarly, is linked to traditions as well. Every form of art has its origin in some sort of ritual or ritualistic performance which later came to be closely linked to a particular religion. Thus, art gained its cult value, which is also its use-value. The mechanical reproduction of art, however, detached art from its tradition or from the ritual. Thus, mechanical reproduction emancipated art from the rituals and, instead, gave it a political function.

Benjamin talks of art in relation to two values: the cult value and the exhibition value. The painting of some deity on the walls of an ancient caveman, for example, had both the cult value, linked to magic, as well as exhibition value. The cult value of art can still be found in the sacred temples where the statues are hidden most of the time or are exposed only to a certain section of people like the priests. Mechanical reproduction has emphasized the exhibition value, which has ultimately transformed the ritual function of art into the function of the commodity. For example, the idols of deities, the ritual songs of indigenous people, and so on are easily available and can be bought in abundance.

Benjamin examines closely the dispute about the artistic value of painting and photography, and drama and sound film. He finds the dispute devious and confused. On the one hand, the technology of reproduction like photography and film has deprived art of its autonomy, while on the other, they have served the political and social function by revolutionizing the product of art.

What could be the difference between film and play concerning actors and spectators? Benjamin writes that in a play the actors present the performance directly to the public whereas in a film the performance is presented by the camera. What the spectators see on the screen is not the total view; the camera angles and the focus of the lens censor the performance. The camera takes the role of the spectator while the spectator becomes the critic without experiencing any personal contact with the actor. Aura is always lacking in screen performance because the aura is tied to the presence of the actor in front of the spectators in person. But in film, there is no presence of the actor in front of the spectators, while in theatre it is always the case. Benjamin writes:

> The aura which, on the stage, emanates from Macbeth, cannot be separated for the spectators from that of the actor. However, the singularity of the shot in the studio is that the camera is substituted for the public. Consequently, the aura that envelops the actor vanishes, and with it the aura of the figure he portrays. (1176)

Thus, the 'beautiful semblance' which art in its traditional form was supposed to have has vanished from art with the development of the technology of reproduction.

The screen performance has accelerated commodification not only of art but also of the artist. The film actor's performance is similar to a performance in front of a mirror, only the difference is that the reflection is portable to the cinema, and thereby to the public. The personality of actors becomes something like a cult. But the cult value lies more in his success to give more money to the producers who have invested in his personality and his performance. While talking about the commodification of art he is not unmindful that films can promote revolution through criticism of social conditions and distribution of property.

The technology of reproduction has also raised many people from the status of readers to authors, or from the status of spectators to actors. Cinema has given birth to critics not only from among the elites but also from among the spectators, much in the same way as the newspapers that demand people's opinions have made readers writers. He says that for centuries only a small number of writers wrote for a large number of readers. But with the increasing extension of the press, a great number of readers turned out to be writers. This idea is more meaningful now than at the time of Benjamin. For, social media like Facebook and Twitter have made almost every user a writer of some sort. The visual technologies of reproduction like YouTube have, in a similar way, opened up the path to stardom through performance to almost everyone. Thus, Benjamin finds both advantages as well as disadvantages of the mechanical reproduction of art. The biggest advantage for him is the revolutionary function whereas the biggest disadvantage is the loss of aura.

Benjamin's essay "Author as Producer" deals with the role of an author in society. He begins the essay with an introduction to tendentious authors. He writes that Plato suggested that the poets should be banished from the ideal state. No state since then has completely banished the poet. However, it is found that authors serve the interest of a certain class. The bourgeois writer of entertainment may claim that he is an autonomous author but he is not; he serves the bourgeois class. On the other hand, according to Benjamin, "A more advanced type of writer does recognize this choice. His decision, made on the basis of class struggle, is to side with the proletariat. This puts an end to his autonomy. His activity is now decided by what is useful to the proletariat in the struggle" (79). Such authors he says are tendentious authors.

Benjamin talks about the long-standing debate of correct political line versus quality regarding a literary work. One might say that the work that has a correct political line does not need to have any other qualities, or one might say that the work must have other literary qualities along with its correct political line. He finds the latter correct. He writes, "The tendency of a literary work can be politically correct only if it is also literarily correct. That is to say, the politically correct tendency includes a literary tendency"(80). He explains that the literary tendency correctly applied, explicitly or implicitly into the political tendency constitutes the quality of a literary work.

Benjamin explains why he chose to write about tendency and quality instead of writing about form and content. He writes that the debate of the relationship between form and content would have been something like an attempt to explain literary connections undialectically. The dialectical approach, for him, would be to insert the literary work into the living social contexts. Living social context involves the relations of production. The often-raised question is about the attitude of a literary work to the relations of production; whether the work accepts them and is reactionary, or aims at overthrowing them and is revolutionary. Instead of this question, he poses another question- what the position of literary work is in the relations of production. This question, he says, is concerned with both the function and the technique of literary work. The term technique involves the social analyses of a literary work, a dialectical starting point to surpass the antithesis between form and content, and the determination of the relationship between tendency and quality.

The technique is related to production. The question is whether, like the farmers and factory laborers, the authors and intellectuals can be producers, or, as Plato believes they are just idle dreamers.

To justify how the authors can be producers, Benjamin presents Sergei Tretiakov's distinction between the operating writer and the informing writer. Talking about the operating writer, Benjamin writes, "His mission is not to report but to struggle; not to play spectator but to intervene actively. He defines this mission in the account he gives of his own activity" (82). Tretiakov proved himself operating author by action, not only in principle. During the collectivization of agriculture in Russia, he went to the 'Communist Lighthouse' commune where he conducted various organizational and promotional works through writing. Moreover, his book *Commanders of the Field* that he wrote after these activities became a milestone in promoting collective agriculture.

It may appear, he says, that the task performed by Tretiakov was that of a journalist or a propagandist and that it had almost nothing to do with literature. But the example of Tretiakov shows, for Benjamin, how comprehensive the literary horizon is being. For, the change in form and genre is dependent on the relations of production. He writes:

> There were not always novels in the past, and there will not always have to be; there have not always been tragedies or great epics. Not always were the forms of commentary, translation, indeed even so-called plagiarism playthings in the margins of literature; they had a place not only in the philosophical but also in the literary writings of Arabia and China. Rhetoric has not always been a minor form: in antiquity, it put its stamp on large provinces of literature. (82)

Through this survey of change, Benjamin aims at persuading that a mighty recasting of literary forms is taking place, in which many of the popular opposites like the author and the reader may lose their force and assimilate to the dialectical transcendence.

Tretiakov's work was progressive, and he is an example of an author as a producer. But left-wing writers with their politico-literary craft are not revolutionaries. Sometimes, like Activists and New Objectivists, they may turn to be counter-revolutionary due to lack of the function of a producer, although they have solidarity with the proletariat in their attitude. Activists and New Objectivists claimed themselves to be socialist, but their definition of socialism was undialectical. They denounced class antagonism to be a driving force behind the establishment of socialism and replaced materialistic dialectics with the notion of common sense. Their biggest flaw was that they preferred the rule of the intellectuals, what they called logocracy, but they were not concerned with the position of the intellectuals in the relation and the process of production.

The author as a producer, says Benjamin, performs certain organizing functions. He writes not only about the products but about the means of production as well. His work is, however, not merely the fascist propaganda works. It adopts correct political tendencies and inculcates literary qualities. This way, the author as a producer teaches other writers and shows the correct path. Such authors can produce more authors, for, they, through instruction and direction, and through the use of improved technique, turn the mere readers and spectators into producers.

# VII

# Max Horkheimer and Theodor W. Adorno, and the Critique of Mass Culture

Horkheimer and Adorno's essay "The Culture Industry; Enlightenment as Mass Deception" discusses the effects of the culture industry and mass culture. While Benjamin finds the mass culture to have positive political consequences, Horkheimer and Adorno find it to be infective. For them, the apparatuses of culture like films, radio, and magazines are no longer art. Their production is mere trash legitimized as a business. Art has been changed into the industry, which is homogenizing every branch of culture. The culture industry has done away with the unique distinctions between the universal and particular, microcosm and macrocosm, and so on. They have been fused together with identical homogeneity. They say, "Each branch of culture is unanimous within itself and all are unanimous together"(94). The apartments in the cities and the bungalows in the outskirts are proof of homogeneity much in the same way as music and film.

The culture industry, like any other industry, under capitalism, is also an apparatus of domination and exploitation. They are monopolized by the capitalists and are used as apparatus of bourgeois hegemony. That is to say, the power of technology over society means the power of those whose economic power is the strongest in society. Radio, films, and magazines propagate and promote the bourgeois ideology. The audience has nothing to do but act as a passive consumer. They cannot resist the ideas propagated by the speakers on the radio or the actors in a film. Their claim that "Technical rationality today is the rationality of domination"(95) is evident in the fact that the culture industry today has destroyed the unique cultures of many ethnic indigenous minorities, and, instead, has installed the cultures of the dominant groups among them.

The culture industry schematically creates a hierarchy by mass-producing different products for different social and economic groups. Consumers are divided into many groups based on their economic condition but the fact is that the mechanically differentiated products are ultimately the same. The differences between individual films, short stories, music, and even cars today are just illusionary. The differences between the more expensive and cheaper product of the same company are narrowing down. For example, the difference between the cars of the same company is marked by the number of cylinders and engine capacity. The difference between films in a similar way is marked by the film stars, expense on technology, costumes, and so on. It is more evident in the fact that many films these days are remade and dubbed.

The culture industry has robbed the audience, listeners, and readers of their logic and imagination. This task is fulfilled schematically by producing identical objects and propagating identical formulas. The spectators in a cinema, for example, do not need to wait till the end to know who will be punished and who will be rewarded. It is almost the same with music, short stories, and soap operas. These products are part of business, the commodities, and the audience or the spectators are reduced merely to consumers, or rather passive consumers. They have almost no part to play except consuming what is sold to them. They have their own choice but what is chosen is not different from the one that is rejected. For, they follow the same formula. The consumers cannot even classify the products, since the classification has already been done by the schematism of production. The sound films and their producers have been the basic guides of society today. Everything needs to pass through the filter of the films and other culture industries. For the moviegoers, the world outside becomes the seamless extension of the world shown in the films.

The culture industry produces sameness both in style and content. Newness is excluded. The machine, that is the apparatus of cultural products rotates on the same spot. New content and style are rejected since they are untried. It has nothing to do with art since it is part of the business. Whatever is demanded and gets a market is produced and sold. The culture industry demands tempo and dynamism, but the motion it talks about is worthless since it does not accept change. The culture industry claims to have taken amusement to the new zenith but, they argue, amusement existed before the industry itself. Then it was rather aesthetic amusement. The mass culture has offered amusement but at the cost of the destruction of serious art, through mockery and pranks. Such a type of amusement congeals into boredom since there is no need for effort to gain such amusement. It merely cheats the consumers by promising them pleasure but the method of amusement is pornographic and prudish. By exposing the objects of desire like the breasts under the sweater and the naked torso, the films merely goad the unsublimated anticipation of pleasure and reduce love merely to romance.

Freedom is another promise of capitalism. But in the age of culture industry freedom is just an abstract concept. People are bound by opinions foreign to them. The culture industry propagates the opinions of the capitalist, the investor, and the producers. The mass, the proletariat, has no role to play in the production. They are mere consumers. Thus, people may think but the thinking is not spontaneous. They do not generate new ideas but just reiterate the same in line with the thought propagated by the culture industry.

The culture industry sells lie as far as amusement and freedom are concerned, and it is the same with tragedy as well. They write, "just as totalitarian society does not abolish the suffering of its members, but registers and plans it, mass culture does the same with tragedy" (122). The industry borrows the tragic substance from art and mocks it. The tragic hero in the past was the one who went against the cosmos and nature of things. Tragedy, therefore, had dignity. But the culture industry has reduced tragedy to mere punishment to those who go against the bourgeois system of production and ideology. Tragedy in late capitalism is a moral threat. The industry portraits suffering but the real dignity of tragedy is always lacking.

The culture industry in late capitalism has reduced individuals to very insignificant details. The films and soap operas and radios are converting man into identical beings like the mass-produced goods with similar dress up, makeup, and tone of speech. Individuality is denied since the individuals are compelled to imitate the imperatives of the system. Capitalism employs the mass culture to indoctrinate the capitalist system into the individuals, and, thus, has disintegrated their psyche by putting them in a state of illusion through various lies. The culture industry has adopted the status of authority. It expresses its commitment to individual freedom and individuality, but in essence, what is offered is pseudo-freedom and pseudo individuality. They thus explain:

> Pseudo individuality is a precondition for apprehending and detoxifying in tragedy: only because individuals are none but mere intersections of universal tendencies is it possible to reabsorb them smoothly into the universal. Mass culture thereby reveals the fictitious quality which has characterized the individual throughout the bourgeois era and is wrong only in priding itself on this murky harmony between universal and particular. The principle of individuality was contradictory from the outset. First, no individuation was ever really achieved. The class-determined form of self-preservation maintained everyone at the level of mere species being. Every bourgeois character expressed the same thing, even and especially when deviating from it: the harshness of competitive society. The individual, on whom society was supported, itself before society's taint; in the individual's, apparent freedom he was the product of society's economic and social apparatus. (125)

They believe that the advance of bourgeois society and bourgeois ideals have promoted the development of the individual but the progress in individuation is the destruction of individuality, which has been reduced today to the competition to achieve individual purposes alone. Society has been fractured and the individual has been broken into pieces. Because of the fragmentation of the individual in capitalism man is at odds with himself and with everyone.

What has Enlightenment to do with all this? What is the significance of the title of the essay? Horkheimer and Adorno mean to say that enlightenment's over-emphasis on an individual's reason has explored various territories of knowledge. It killed the old worldview and gave birth to a new mode of thinking. Mass culture is also a logical development of enlightenment. The enlightenment's demand of individual freedom and use of reason are contradictory at the phase of mass culture since the culture industry has made individuals devoid of freedom as well as reason. The operation of the negative dialectic of enlightenment shows that it is bound to go against itself. Its emphasis on reason has been mocked by its own development. For example, liberalism, capitalism, individualism, and culture industry are all the by-products of enlightenment, the last of which, however, forbids freedom. Therefore, they consider enlightenment to be a mass deception.

# VIII

# Christopher Caudwell, Poetry and Historical Materialism

Christopher Caudwell gives a materialistic account of the origin of poetry in *Illusion and Reality*. Poetry in the earlier days was not differentiated from other literary genres. The early literature like history, religion, magic, or law was preserved in poetical form. They were metrical compositions with the use of rhyme. Though they were poetical in form, they were not so entirely in the sense we use today. The language, for him, was, instead, a heightened form of ordinary language with the use of meter and other decorum. In the early stages, such heightened language was usually accompanied by music and dance.

For Caudwell, poetry is not anything like racial, national, genetic, or specific in its essence, but as something economic. Its development is based on the division of labor. Poetry, he says, in its earliest days, had nothing to do with aesthetic standards. Rather, it was such quality that was "associated only with division and organization of labor" (15). In the early days of hunting and gathering, very limited differentiation existed depending only on age, sex, and totem. Similarly, their art and language were not differentiated. Thus, poetry or the heightened language was a common medium of collective wisdom, and that it is more natural than other genres like a novel. About the language of poetry, its connection with society, and its difference from the novel, he writes:

> We cannot help noticing already the connection of early poetry – poetry which is also tribal wisdom and rude chronology – with a state of society in which economic differentiation due to division of labor hardly exists. In primitive society man's genetic individuality realizes itself simply like a physical trait – a wide forehead or a splay foot. Remembering that there seems in all ages something simple and direct about poetry, that good poetry can be written by the comparatively immature, that it has a more personal and emotional core than other forms of literary art, we may already guess that poetry expresses in a special manner the genetic instinctive part of the individual, as opposed, say, to the novel, which expresses the individual as an adapted type, as a social character, as the man realized in society. Such an art form as the novel could therefore only arise in a society where economic differentiation gives such scope for the realization of individual differences that it is useful and valuable to tackle man, the individual, from this angle. There is no essential difference; it is a difference of aspect. But it is an important difference and one to which we will return again and again. In this sense, poetry is the child of Nature, just as the developed novel is the child of the sophistication of modern culture. (18)

Literature, for him, is the union of genetic individualities and social differentiation which unites best in the genres like tragedy, dramatic verse, and epic, because these genres flourish at the time of rapidly changing society. He gives an example of great works like *Odysseus, Oedipus*, and *Hamlet* which are the product of growing new social and economic differentiation at the period of change.

Poetry, he says, was born among primitive hunters and gatherers in the form of charm, prayer, and history. This heightened language lived through ages accompanied by music, dance, and gesture changing gradually into tradition and culture. Gradually it went through differentiation: as different new class types like the priests, lawyers, administrators, and soldiers arose from the primitive undifferentiated society, the heightened language of the primitive gatherers and hunters split into science, history, theology, law, economics, and so on. For example, the earlier books on law, religion, or history available till today are written in poetic form. However, it does not mean that the earlier language as a whole was the heightened rhythmic language; the non-rhythmic language too existed side by side. While the heightened rhythmic language was used as the collective speech for expressing public emotion, the everyday non-rhythmic language was used for private persuasion.

For Caudwell, poetry grows out of the economic life of the tribe, and illusion grows out of reality:

> Unlike the life of beasts, the life of the simplest tribe requires a series of efforts which are not instinctive, but which are demanded by the necessities of a non-biological economic aim – for example, a harvest. Hence the instincts must be harnessed to the needs of the harvest by a social mechanism. An important part of this mechanism is the group festival, the matrix of poetry, which frees the stores of emotion and canalizes them in a collective channel. The real object, the tangible aim – a harvest – becomes in the festival a phantastic object. The real object is not here now. The phantastic object is here now – in phantasy. As man by the violence of the dance, he screams of the music and the hypnotic rhythm of the verse is alienated from present reality, which does not contain the unsown harvest, so he is projected into the phantastic world in which these things phantastically exist. That world becomes more real, and even when the music dies away the ungrown harvest has a greater reality for him, spurring him on to the labors necessary for its accomplishment. (23)

The primitive tribe collected the collective emotion in words, carefully selected and woven into a rhythmical and metrical association that they chanted in every feast and function that were part of their economic life. The art sweetened their work. However, with the increasing division of labor, poetry gradually began to stand in opposition to labor and the poet began to be a solitary man:

> The increasing division of labor, which includes also its increasing organization, seems to produce a movement of poetry away from concrete living, so that art appears to be in opposition to work, a creation of leisure. The poet is typically now the solitary individual; his expression, the lyric. The division of labor has led to a class society, in which consciousness has gathered at the pole of the ruling class, whose rule eventually produces the conditions for idleness. Hence art ultimately is completely separated from work, with disastrous results to both, which can only be healed by the ending of classes. (24)

Thus, art, for him, was born out of collective emotion and collective labor and, consequently, it is, by origin, an economic activity. He appears to be outrightly refusing the notion of art for art's sake. For him, the truth of poetry lies not in its abstract statement but in its dynamic role in society, i.e., its content of collective emotion.

He writes that the collective emotion of the tribe which we call poetry gave birth to religion, the collective phantasy that is deviated from the material world of terrestrial life which is the original matrix of poetry. He gives a brief account of the historical development of religion out of poetry. Religion was conceived first as mythology which shared many properties of poetry. For example, it was still organic and it still expressed the collective emotion. But gradually mythology began to ossify and religion emerged out of it. But the religion was neither organic nor expressed the collective emotion, rather it created a class society. As a result, the undifferentiated tribal life ended with the end of mythology. The division of undifferentiated tribes into the hostile classes of the ones who exercised thought and the other ones who only worked is reflected in religion and art as well. Religion and art, with the division of classes, ceased to be the collective product of the tribe and became a product of the ruling class that imposed it on the ruled ones.

Poetry before the bourgeois economy came into dominance, used to have its social function. Even Milton, Keats, Shelley, and Wordsworth realized that poet had a social function like that of a teacher or a prophet. But in the bourgeois economy, poetry, like anything thought to be sacred, turns to be a commodity; and the poet, who is thought to be the inspired one, turns to be a producer for an anonymous free market. Moreover, Caudwell recognizes the revolutionary role of the poets. He says that in a revolutionary period, culture expresses the aspirations of the revolution or the doubts of the dispossessed. He believes that Plato's idea of banishing poets from his Ideal Republic was such doubt of the dispossessed. For, Plato wants to establish the republic of the aristocrats at a time when the aristocracy was dying and new classes were emerging in Greece. Concerning Plato's idea on the suppression of the poets, Caudwell calls him a fascist philosopher; and concerning his idea of poetry emerging out of the divine inspiration, he calls him Athenian Hegel.

He believes that poetry in the modern bourgeois world has taken the opposite course of what it adhered to on its onset. The sacred thing that was born out of the tribal celebrations and festivals to express the collective emotion has now been anti poetic as the bourgeois poet has turned to become an individualist. He writes:

> The bourgeois poet sees himself as an individualist striving to realize what is most essentially himself by an expansive outward movement of the energy of his heart, by a release of internal forces which outward forms are crippling. This is the bourgeois dream, the dream of the one man alone producing the phenomena of the world. He is Faust, Hamlet, Robinson Crusoe, Satan, and Prufrock. (50)

Caudwell presents a survey of the development of poetry through different ages to trace the connection between poetry and economy.

In the transitional period between feudalism and capitalism, the condition for the growth of the bourgeois class was created lawlessly. The bourgeois felt that his instincts what he called freedom, were restrained by laws and that he wanted to obtain them by the violent expansion of his desires. The literature of the Elizabethan age reflects such desires for instincts as seen in Marlowe's Faust and Tamburlaine. Such a life principle of the expansion of individual will reaches its highest embodiment in the renaissance "Prince", and also in Shakespeare's tragedies, all of which have princely heroes, and in all of them, the kingly values are lauded as the ideal values.

Poetry until the age of primitive accumulation had not lost its collective value. Shakespeare for example expressed the public life of the court. In his dramas, he lived with his audience. His works were not individualistic and he was not a producer for some bourgeois market. In this period the elaborate division of labor had not taken place, and, consequently, culture, art, and language were not differentiated. This undifferentiated language was used at the dawn of the bourgeois development to express the collective emotion of the court.

By the time of Milton, the voices of revolution began to be heard. It was the era of the bourgeois revolution against the monarchy and the privileged nobility in the name of parliament and liberty. Milton himself came up with revolutionary poetry- revolutionary both in style and content. As Shakespeare stood for the monarchy, Milton stood for the people.

The industrial revolution, which he calls the explosive stage of capitalism, made the poet detach himself from society. The revolution made the poet an "individualist realizing only the instincts of his heart and not responsible to society's demands - whether expressed in the duties of a citizen, a fearer of God, or a faithful servant of Mammon" (73). The poets in this period were revolutionary, or rather mirror revolutionary, in that they went away from reality, seeking the expression of the instincts, personal emotion, and the so-called freedom, shattering the change of society. Blake, Byron, Keats, Wordsworth, and Shelley express bourgeois ideologies in their own ways. The industrial revolution that created a condition of commodity fetishism affected the poets as well. In art, the equivalent of the commodity-fetishism came in the form of "art for art's sake". It made the bourgeois poet a producer for the free market. Such a commodity-fetishism in art separated the world of art from the world of reality. And also, it separated the art from its source. The poet finds himself in a market competing freely with other commodities. The bourgeois invention of the printing press and the bourgeois expansion through colonization has made the poet produce commodities for the market that, otherwise, he was unknown of. The bourgeois economy that made a poet a mere producer and his poem a commodity has ultimately turned the poet to be an outdated artist:

> The poet is the most craft of writers. His art requires the highest degree of technical skill of any artist, and it is precisely this technical skill that is not wanted by the vast majority of people in developed capitalism. He is as out of date as a medieval stone-carver in an era of plaster casts. As the virtual proletarianization of society increases, the conditions of men's work, robbed of spontaneity, more and more make them demand a mass-produced "low-brow" art, whose flatness and shallowness serve to adapt them to their unfreedom. The poet becomes a "high-brow," a man whose skill is not wanted. It becomes too much trouble for the average man to read poetry. (90)

At such a condition, the poet reacts against the bourgeois mode of production as did the craftsman by setting the craft skill in opposition to a social function, i.e., art in opposition to life itself. This reaction develops ultimately into surrealism, which, for him, is the last bourgeois revolutionary movement. This revolutionary, the surrealist, is politically an anarchist who demands complete personal freedom and destruction of all social relations.

# IX

# Louis Althusser and the Study of Ideology

Louis Althusser dispersedly presents his ideas on art and literature. His ideas on the role of ideologies can be important for a student of Marxist literary criticism. Though not elaborate to the fullest, he gives a hint of his position in the matter related to art and literature in his letter to Andre Daspre. In the letter, he talks about the relationship between art and ideology, a popular subject for Marxist critics for years. He does not rank real art among the ideologies but finds a specific relationship between art and ideology. He writes that art means making us see, perceive or feel something which alludes to reality; and for him, "What art makes us see, and therefore gives to us in the form of 'seeing', 'perceiving' and 'feeling' (. . . ), is the ideology from which it is born, in which it bathes, from which it detaches itself as art; and to which it alludes" (A Letter 1480).

These observations about the relationship between art and ideology lead him to the distinction between art and science. He writes that authentic art does not give knowledge as it merely makes us see, feel or perceive. But what art gives us maintains a specific relation to knowledge. Art, he says, makes us see the ideology from which it is born. Artists, like the novelists, do not give any knowledge of the world they describe but make the readers perceive the lived experience of the individual, i.e., the reality of the ideology of that world. Science, on the other hand, deals with an abstraction of structure which is opposed to the 'lived experience' and the 'individual'. Ideology, the lived experience, and the individual are also the object of science but, unlike art, science deals with them differently. The object of art and science may be the same, but they give us the same thing in a different form. While art presents them in the form of seeing, perceiving, or feeling, science presents them in the form of knowledge.

Althusser's idea of how ideologies are inculcated (the idea he talks about while analyzing the process of the reproduction of the productive force) can also be useful for a student of literary criticism. His idea of schools and other institutions as well as state apparatuses, including ideology, echoes Gramsci's idea of the methods of hegemony. He says that besides teaching scientific and literary cultures, schools teach students", the rules of good behavior, that is, the properties to be observed by every agent in the division of labor, depending on the post he is 'destined' to hold in it" (*On the Reproduction* 51). These rules, he says, are the rules of respect and the rules, of dominion. Schools inculcate ideologies of subjugation to the would-be laborers and the ideologies of dominion to the would-be capitalist. The idea of the use of proper language serves that end by preparing the would-be capitalist and their underlings to con the workers. Thus, along with the reproduction of labor-power, the school reproduces the labor-power's submission to the dominant ideology.

Althusser's views on the ideology that he presents in the analysis of the Marxian metaphor of base and superstructure can be useful not only to understand society and social relations but also to analyze literary works as the latter is always a product of a particular society in a given time. In the metaphor of a two-storeyed building, the bottom, or the base, stands for the productive forces and the relations of production whereas the upper floor or the superstructure stands for the political, legal, and ideological phenomena. Althusser divides the superstructure into two levels: the legal-political superstructure (law and state) and the ideological superstructure (various ideologies).

Law he says is essentially repressive by nature for the simple reason that it does not exist in the absence of a corresponding system of sanctions. He writes, "On the one hand, it rests on part of the state repressive apparatus for support. On the other hand, it rests on legal ideology and a little supplement of moral ideology for support" (68). By state repressive apparatus, he means the institutions like the army and police while moral ideology refers to the code of discipline and decency. The legal ideology for him stands for people's behavior of respect for the law. The legal ideologies are related, but not identical, to law.

Similarly, the state is a repressive apparatus for the reason that it enables the dominant classes to ensure their domination over the working class. The term state, that Althusser calls state apparatus, covers all the legal practices, the army, the government, and the administration. Alongside the repressive state apparatuses, he discusses the ideological state apparatuses that the ruling class sets up for domination over the ruled. These ideological state apparatuses are, he lists, the scholastic, the familial, the religious, the political, the associative, the information and news, the publishing and distribution, and the cultural apparatuses. Each of these ideological state apparatuses is correspondent to certain institutions or organizations which create a system that the individuals follow. For example, the scholastic apparatus is correspondent to schools, the political apparatus to political parties, and so on. Thus, he classifies state apparatuses between repressive state apparatus and ideological state apparatus. While repressive state apparatus makes direct or indirect physical violence, the ideological state apparatus does not use physical violence. The objective of both of them however is the same, i.e., to ensure domination by the ruling class over the ruled ones.

Althusser clarifies whether or not the private institutions belong to the state apparatus. He believes that the private institutions owned by individuals, like those owned by the state, function as a component of the ideological state apparatus. They function under the direction of the state ideology, in the service of the state's politics and the dominant class. They cannot promote their own ideology which is opposed to the state ideology. But the private institutions, correspondent to various ideological apparatuses, too, belong to the state apparatuses.

He argues that the state apparatuses play a double role, i.e., while the state apparatus plays the role of ideological state apparatus, the latter too plays the role of the former. For example, the army, the repressive state apparatus, trains its recruits both by repression and inculcation of ideology. That means sometimes they use violence, and sometimes the method of discussion and persuasion. Similarly, schools, the ideological state apparatuses, train the school children not only by various methods of teaching but also by the methods of punishment, whether physical or moral.

He believes that the apparatuses set up by the old bourgeois regime must be destroyed. He says, "It is not enough to destroy the repressive apparatus; it is also necessary to destroy and replace the Ideological State Apparatuses. New ones have to be put in place, urgently; otherwise - . . . - the very future of the revolution will be jeopardized" (90). He is not unmindful that the task is arduous and takes a lot of time. But it must be accomplished for avoiding political compromises and to construct socialism. To accomplish this goal, first, a comprehensive plan is needed- a plan that explains what new systems should be invented and how they should be implemented. Then competent personnel loyal to the revolution should be trained to apply the new revolutionary proletarian ideology in each of the ideological state apparatuses set up by the proletarian regime.

In the period of capitalism Althusser argues, the school has been the dominant ideological state apparatus. In the pre-capitalist period, this position was occupied by the church. Revolutionary bourgeois knew it and therefore, concentrated on the anti-clerical and anti-religious struggle. He, thus, writes:

> The main objective and result of the French Revolution was not just to transfer state power from the feudal aristocracy to the mercantile capitalist bourgeoisie, destroy part of the old Repressive State Apparatus, and put a new one in its place (for example, the national popular army), but also to attack the number-one Ideological State Apparatus, the Church. Hence the civil constitution of the clergy, the confiscation of church property, and the creation of new Ideological State Apparatuses to replace the religious Ideological State Apparatus in its dominant role. (143)

The capitalist bourgeois used the school to ensure ideological hegemony much in the same way as the aristocracy in the pre-capitalist period used the church.

Thus, Althusser analyzes the state apparatuses dividing them into two types: the ideological state apparatuses and the repressive state apparatuses. He believes that while the repressive state apparatuses include the state organizations like the army and the police that use force to repress the subjects, the ideological state apparatuses include the organizations like schools, churches, religions, and other cultural organizations that use persuasion, hegemony, and other techniques of discipline and pacifying. The purpose of both types of state apparatuses, however, is the same, i.e., to suppress and rule the subjects. Althusser's belief that even the privately-owned institutions belong to the state apparatuses is a novel thought in Marxism. He explains that as the ideologies carried by such privately-owned institutions are tantamount to those carried by the state-owned ideologies, and as no privately-owned institution can practice ideologies without the approval of the state, the ideologies of the privately-owned institutions are also the ideologies of the state.

# X

# Raymond Williams and the Materialistic Interpretation of Culture

At a time when the Marxist critical tradition studied art, literature, language, and culture as dependent on the material base, Williams comes up with new ideas regarding the development of these human phenomena and their place in society. In his book, *Marxism and Literature,* which presents himself as both a critic of Marxism and a developer of the Marxist theory, he deals with each of these concepts systematically only to establish the relation between Marxism, both theory as well as practice, and literature.

The concept of culture, he believes, is at the center of modern thought and practice. As the concept of culture evolved through a number of contradictions, it fuses, in it, those contradictory experiences and tendencies. Cultural analyses, therefore, is impossible without the historical consciousness of the concept itself. Culture as a concept, like society and economy, is a recent historical formation. Before it gained its new meaning, it was understood as "the growth and tending of crops and animals, and by extension the growth and tending of human faculties" (11). Similarly, society, once known as an active fellowship, has come to mean a general system or order; and economy, the management of household and community, is defined today as the entire system of production distribution and exchange.

The culture, he writes, meant the same as a civilization in the late 18$^{th}$ century. Beginning with Rousseau on through the romantic movement, however, the signification of civilization and culture began to be different. While civilization was viewed as an external development that is intrinsically linked to the concept of society, culture was viewed as an inner or spiritual process of subjectivity and imagination. He, thus, writes, "Culture, or more specifically art and literature (themselves newly generalized and abstracted), were seen as the deepest record, the deepest impulse, and the deepest resource of the human spirit" (15). That meant, for him, culture was the secularization and the liberalization of the earlier metaphysical forms.

Meanwhile, culture underwent another development, i.e., the idea of culture as an anthropological and sociological concept. This sense of culture is rooted in the Enlightenment's emphasis on reason that can "create higher forms of the social and natural order, overcoming ignorance and superstition and the social and political forms to which they have led and which they support" (16). Culture, thus, before Marxism intervened, came to be known as an inner process characterized by intellectual life and arts. Marxism, he believes, analyzed human civilization as a specific historical form. For example, the bourgeois society was created by the capitalistic mode of production. Marxism, he believes, has offered a new revolutionary idea about the development of culture as a product of economic activities. Williams, however, has certain reservations regarding the Marxist notion of culture as belonging to the "realm of 'mere' ideas, beliefs, arts, customs, determined by the basic material history" (19). He means to say that since cultural history is essentially material in nature, Marxism should rethink the cultural theory beyond the argument of base and superstructure - an argument that separates culture from material social life, much in the same way as the idealist cultural thought does. Also, he believes that the first stage of Marxism missed the question of human language that was decisive in the development of the concept of culture.

Language, Williams writes, has been an intrinsic part of human life. A definition of language, for him, is the definition of human beings as well. Such an important category, which constructs all other major categories like, world, reality, nature, human, and the category 'language' itself, however, has not got much space in Marxism. He suggests that Marxism can better forward the study of language with the proposition that language is an activity, like any economic activity, and that it is a historical phenomenon. The major emphasis on language as an activity, he says, began in the 18th century. The idealistic view of language that stood on the foundation of Plato's ideas had separated language and reality.

There have been attempts to link language and reality, and to study language as an event in Marxism, particularly by Marx and Engels themselves, who, in a chapter on Feuerbach in the German ideology, have written that language is a practical consciousness that arises from the necessity of intercourse with other people. Thus, since language developed at some point in evolutionary history. It is to be seen "as a persistent kind of creation and recreation; a dynamic presence and a constant regenerative process" (31). This concept of language as a practical and constitutive activity, essentially a social activity intrinsically tied to every other human activity, was overshadowed by the orthodox Marxism that placed language in the superstructure. And that the idea of language as an activity was threatened by the declaration of Stalin who maintained that "language did not have any class character but rather a national character" (34).

Such theories, however, were opposed in the 1920s by the emerging Marxist linguists. The opposition, Raymond says, is best represented in V. N. Volosinov's *Marxism and the Philosophy of Language*, in which Volosinov reconsidered the problem of language within a general Marxist orientation that "enabled him to see activity (. . .) as a social activity and to see system (. . .) in relation to this activity and not, as had hitherto been the case, formally separated from it " (35). This implies that meaning is necessarily a social action and that it depends on social relationships. For him, consciousness, like meaning, is also a social

81

action that is built on material science. The relation between the formal element of the sign and the meaning is, however, conventional but it is neither arbitrary nor fixed.

Williams believes that Volosinov's ideas on meaning and consciousness have significant relevance to Marxism, but finds his discussion of the sign-system misleading. Sign, he says, has to be revalued to emphasize its variability while the system has to be revalued to emphasize social process rather than fixed sociality. He, thus, concludes that we can add the definition of language development as historically and socially constituting to the definition of language as constitutive. Then, he says, "we can define the changing practical consciousness of human beings, . . ., in the complex variations of actual language use" (43-44). From this theoretical foundation, we can go on to distinguish literature from the abstract concept that reduces it to a mere superstructural by-product of collective labor.

Literature, Williams writes, began to develop to gain its modern form in the renaissance period, and by the 19th century, it had fully developed. Before the transformation, it was, "a specialization of the area formerly categorized as rhetoric and grammar: a specialization to reading and, in the material context of the development of painting, to the printed word and especially the book" (47). Literature then, even until the beginning of the 18th century, stood for its educational value since it bore its social distinction as polite or humane learning. However, with the growing industrial capitalism, literature, like every other concept such as culture and society, underwent a certain transformation: the shift of the idea of learning to taste or sensibility as a criterion defining literary quality; the specialization of literature as a creative or imaginative work; and the emergence of the idea of national literature. The shift of literature from learning to taste or sensibility, according to Williams was related to the division of class. Such concepts were characteristically bourgeois categories and could be applied equally to wine as well.

Like literature, literary criticism too went through a certain transformation. It developed from the commentaries on the literature "to the conscious exercise of taste, sensibility, and discrimination" (49). It was concerned more with the consumption of the works than with their production. Such a transformation of literary criticism is also related to the existing dominant class. He writes:

'Taste' in literature might be confused with 'taste' in everything else, but, within class terms, responses to literature were notably integrated, and the relative integration of the 'reading public' (a characteristic term of the definition) was a sound base for important literary production. The reliance on 'sensibility', as a special form of an attempted emphasis on whole 'human' response, had its evident weaknesses in its tendency to separate 'feeling' from 'thought' (with an associated vocabulary of 'subjective' and 'objective', 'unconscious' and ' conscious', 'private' and 'public'). At the same time, it served, at its best, to insist on 'immediate' and 'living' substance (in which its contrast with the 'learned' tradition was especially marked). It was really only as this class lost its relative cohesion and dominance that the weakness of the concepts as concepts became evident. And it is evidence of at least its residual hegemony that criticism, taken as a new conscious discipline into the universities, to be practiced by what became a new para-national profession, retained these founding class concepts, alongside attempts to establish new abstractly objective criteria. More seriously, criticism was taken to be a natural definition of literary studies, themselves defined by the specializing category (printed works of a certain quality) of literature. Thus, these forms of the concepts of literature and criticism are, in the perspective of historical social development, forms of a class specialization and control of general social practice, and of a class limitation of the questions which it might raise. (49)

For Williams, the specialization of literature to creative or imaginative work is a response to the repressive tendency of industrial capitalism. Along with the shift of art from something meaning human skill to something defined by imagination and sensibility, aesthetics and fiction too gained new meanings. While aesthetics shifted from its sense of general perception to the specialized category of something beautiful and artistic, fiction and myth, which we looked upon as fancies and lies, began to bear the new meaning of imaginative truth. Similarly, romance and romantic

83

too gained new positive emphasis. These were the vital changes that literature and literary criticism went through. Even Marxism, which emphasizes practical consciousness, has shown very little effort against such changes that have sent literature to the realm of imagination and sensibility. The later Marxist tradition attempted to apply the practical consciousness in three ways: first, it attempted to assimilate literature to ideology; second, it attempted to include 'the literature of the people' into the literary tradition; and third, it attempted to relate literature to the social and economic history within which it had been produced. The first one, for him, is merely an extension of tradition, but the last two attempts are significant ones. For half a century, significant tendencies in Marxist literary criticism have been developed by the critics like Lukacs, the Frankfurt school, and the like but they are not sufficient. For him, the recognition of literature as a social and historical category is the most crucial theoretical break in the field of Marxist literary criticism.

Williams believes that Marxism's ideas on creativity are different from other systems of thought as most systems of thought emphasized human activity as derived from an external cause like the god, animal inheritance, permanent instinctual systems, and so on. Marxism, in a contrast, believes in the idea of human creativity or self-creation. However, he is not satisfied with what Marxism has done so far. For him, Marxism has not yet succeeded in making creativity specific, in the full social and historical material process. He says:

> It is not only that some important variants of Marxism have moved in opposite directions, reducing creative practice to representation, reflection, or ideology. It is also that Marxism, in general, has continued to share, in an abstract way, an undifferentiated and in that form metaphysical celebration of creativity, even alongside these practical reductions. (206)

For him, the literary texts, the characters in them, the plot, theme, and the like are not creations, in the strictest sense of the word. Rather what we call creation is merely a kind of social extension. For example, a character in a certain novel or a play, instead of being a creation, may have been copied from life or adopted from an existing book. That is to say, the creation of characters is a kind of tagging of name, sex, occupation, physical quality, and so on. Thus, for him, "the real literary process is active reproduction" in which "the 'persons' are 'created' to show that people are 'like this' and their relations 'like this'" (209). Literary or artistic creation, from this perspective, is inseparable from the material social process, and cannot simply be banished into the realm of abstract ideology.

## Works Cited

Althusser, Louis. *"A Letter on Art in Reply to Andre Daspre".* *The Norton Anthology of Theory and Criticism.* Ed. V. B. Leitch. New York: Norton, 2001. 1480-1483. Print.

- - -. *On the Reproduction of Capitalism: Ideology and Ideological State Apparatuses.* Trans. G. M. Goshgarin. London: Verso: 1995. Print.

Benjamin, Walter. "The Author as Producer". *The Work of Art in the Age of Its Technological Reproducibility, and Other Writings on Media.* Cambridge: Belknap Press of Harvard University Press, 2008. 92-108. Web.

- - -. *"*The Work of Art in the Age of Mechanical Reproduction*".* *The Norton Anthology of Theory and Criticism.* Ed. V. B. Leitch. New York: Norton, 2001. 1166-1185. Print.

Caudwell, Christopher. *Illusion and Reality: A Study of the Sources of Poetry.* Bombay: People's Publishing House Ltd, 1947. Print.

Engels, Friedrich. "Letter to J. Bloch". *K. Marx F. Engels V. Lenin: A Collection on Historical Materialism.* Moscow: Progress Publishers, 1972. 294-296. Print.

Gramsci, Antonio. *Selections from the Prison Notebooks of Antonio Gramsci:* Ed. Quintin Hoare and Geoffrey Nowell

Smith. 1<sup>st</sup> ed. New York: International Publishers, 1971.
Print.

Horkheimer, Max and Theodor W. Adorno. "The Culture
Industry: Enlightenment as Mass Deception". *Dialectic of
Enlightenment: Philosophical Fragments*. Ed. Gunzelin
Schmid Noerr. Trans. Edmund Jephcott. California: Stanford
University Press, 2002. 94-137. Print.

Lenin, Vladimir I. *Tolstoy and His Time*. New York:
International Publishers, 1952. Print.

- - -. *What is to Be Done: Burning Questions of Our Movement*.
New York: International Publishers, 1929. Print.

Lukacs, Georg. "Eulogy for Maxim Gorky: A Great Proletarian
Humanist".
<https://www.marxists.org/archive/lukacs/works/1936/gorky
.htm>

- - -. "Existentialism".
<https://www.marxists.org/archive/lukacs/works/1949/existe
ntialism.htm>

- - -. "Realism in the Balance". *The Norton Anthology of Theory
and Criticism*. Ed. V. B. Leitch. New York: Norton, 2001.
1033–1058. Print.

- - -. "Tagore's Gandhi Novel - Review of Rabindranath Tagore:
The Home and the World".

&lt;https://www.marxists.org/archive/lukacs/works/1922/tagore.htm&gt;

- - -. *The Destruction of Reason*. Atlantic Highlands, N.J: Humanities Press, 1981. Print.

- - -. *The Historical Novel*. London: Merlin Press, 1962. Print.

- - -. *The Theory of the Novel: A Historico-Philosophical Essay on the Forms of Great Epic Literature*. London: Merlin Press, 1971. Print.

Marx, Karl. *Capital: A Critique of Political Economy*. 3 vols. London: Penguin Books, 1976.

- - -. *Economic and Philosophic Manuscripts of 1844*. Amherst, N.Y: Prometheus Books, 1988. Print

- - -. "Preface". *A Contribution to the Critique of Political Economy*. Trans. N. I. Stone. Chicago: Charles H. Kerr & Company, 1904. Print.

Marx, Karl, and Friedrich Engels. *Manifesto of the Communist Party*. New York: International Publishers, 1948. Print.

- - -. *The German Ideology: Including Theses on Feuerbach and Introduction to the Critique of Political Economy*. Amherst, N.Y: Prometheus Books, 1998. Print.

Shaw, Bernard. "Preface". *The Apple Cart: A Political Extravaganza*. London: Constable and Company, 1932. Print.

Trotsky, Leon. *Literature and Revolution*. Chicago, ILL: Haymarket Books, 2009. Print.

Walker, David M, and Daniel Gray. *Historical Dictionary of Marxism*. Lanham, Md: Scarecrow Press, 2007. Print.

Williams, Raymond. *Marxism and Literature*. Oxford: Oxford University Press, 1977. Print.